THE PREHISTORIC ROCK ART OF GALLOWAY & THE ISLE OF MAN

Ronald W.B. Morris

THE PREHISTORIC ROCK ART OF GALLOWAY & THE ISLE OF MAN

BLANDFORD PRESS

First published in U.K. in 1979 by
Blandford Press Ltd., Link House, West Street, Poole, Dorset

Hardcover ISBN 0 7137 0974 X
Paperback ISBN 0 7137 0975 8

Printed and bound by
Butler and Tanner,
Frome, Somerset

CONTENTS

FOREWORD

by JACK G. SCOTT, MA, FMA, FSA Scot,
formerly Keeper, Department of Archaeology, Ethnography
and History, Glasgow Art Gallery and Museum.

The Prehistoric Rock Art of Galloway (with a section on the Isle of Man) is the second of a group of three books by Ronald Morris on the rock carvings – mainly cup-and-ring-marks – of the Neolithic and Bronze Ages in Scotland. The first, *The Prehistoric Rock Art of Argyll* (Dolphin Press, 1977), has already appeared, and the third, to cover the remainder of southern Scotland, is well in hand.

To the professional archaeologist the most refreshing thing about the work of Ronald Morris is his total lack of prejudice or bias. His aim is the accurate presentation of the facts, and his objectivity no doubt stems from his long legal experience. This approach, combined with an infectious enthusiasm and backed by considerable determination (for rock art is not always to be found in the most accessible of places), has produced a formidable body of information.

Of course, most readers would like to know not only where rock art is to be found and what forms it takes but also what it means. As to its meaning, speculation has run riot in the past, and in this book Ronald Morris lists no fewer than one hundred and four varieties of theories and explanations for the making of the carvings, together with his assessment of their credibility.

Somewhere amidst all the theories the truth must lie, and only through fair and accurate presentation of the evidence may progress be made. All of us would like to know more about the carvings. Where Ronald Morris has succeeded is in providing the basic information to enable us to see for ourselves, and to speculate to our hearts' content.

ACKNOWLEDGMENTS

I must first most gratefully acknowledge the financial help which has enabled my field-work on the rock art of Southern Scotland, including this most interesting area of Galloway, to proceed. First of all there were initial grants from the Society of Antiquaries of Scotland and the Ancient Monuments Society, London, which enabled the work to be begun. These were followed by most generous grants by way of a Leverhulme Research Fellowship and a Kodak Award.

Acknowledgement must also most gratefully be made for the very full and accurate information on many of the sites, and much other help given to me by Alastair Maclaren and the Royal Commission on the Ancient and Historical Monuments of Scotland, and as regards the Isle of Man by Frank Cowin; also for much help in accurately 'fixing' and checking the exact position on the map of each site and other information, given me by J. L. Davidson and his staff at the Archaeology Branch (Scotland) of the Ordnance Survey.

I am also indebted to the following, among many others, for help and information on individual sites and other details: the National Museum of Antiquities of Scotland, the Inspectorate of Ancient Monuments of Scotland, the Manx Museum, M. F. Ansell, the late D. C. Bailey, T. R. Collin, W. G. Cubbons, Dr. F. Garrad, E. Hadingham, Major and Mrs. Hannay of Cardroness, Miss A. Henshall, C. Jackson, A. Kennedy, I. F. Macleod, R. McMaster, the late Gavin Maxwell, F. J. Moore, A. Murray, J. Parker, F. J. Radcliffe, Roland Smith, R. B. K. Stevenson, J. D. Stewart, Professor A. Thom, A. E. Truckell and J. Williams.

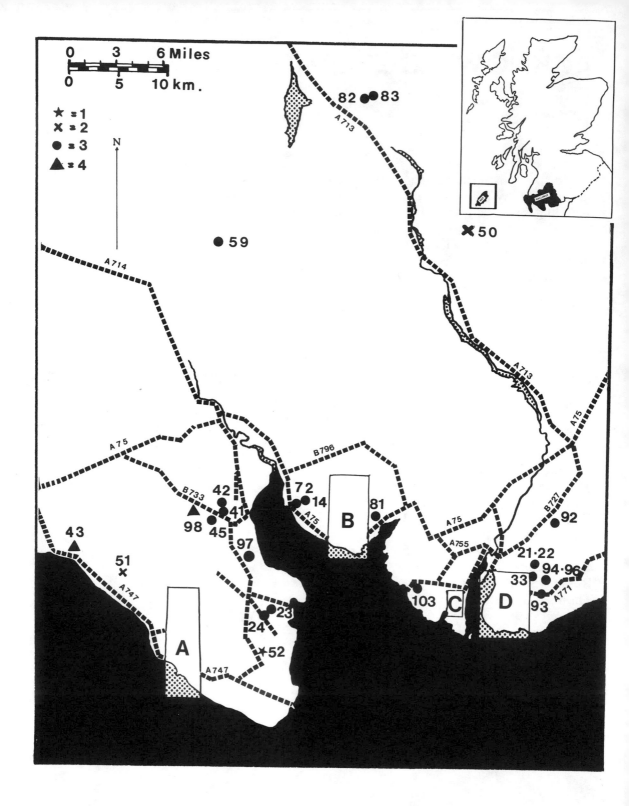

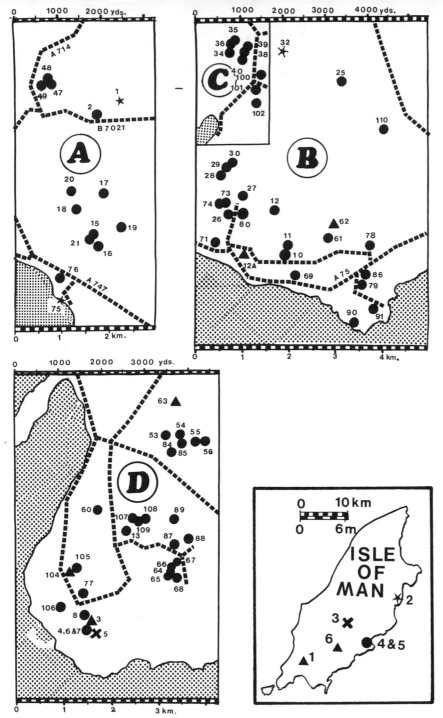

GALLOWAY AND THE ISLE OF MAN — The sites are numbered as in the text and the main access roads are shown. 1 = the carvings include one or more spirals. 2 = they include one or more spirals. 3 = they include cups-and-rings but neither of the above. 4 = other types of carving occur on this site.

The other maps show an enlarged picture of the sections of Galloway marked "A", "B", "C", and "D" on the map opposite. The symbols have the same meaning as on that map.

9

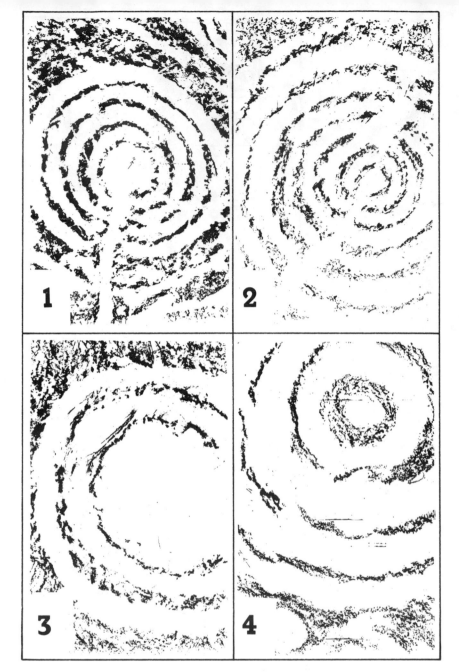

RUBBINGS OF SOME TYPICAL GALLOWAY ROCK CARVINGS.
1. **Broughton Mains 2,** with a radial groove from its cup. 2. **Bombie 1** with an uncommon diametrical groove. 3. **Newlaw Hill 1,** with an extra-large cup, and no groove. 4. **Cairnharrow** — un-gapped rings, with no groove. 5. **Grange 1** — a unique design. 6. **Torrs 3B** — another unique design. 7. **Barholm 2,** its groove comes from the ring only. 8. **Blairbuy 4** — un-gapped single rings. 9. **Gallows Outon** — one of the uncommon spirals. 10. **Balcraig 1** — part of a very big cup-and-ring. 11. **House of Elrig** — an unusual "keyhole" type, here with no central cup. 12. **Glentrool** — carved on a very hard rock surface. 13. **Low Banks 2.** 14. **Kirmabreck** — much narrower rings than usual — perhaps incised, or very lightly pecked. 15. **Blairbuy 3** — the tangental parallel lines are unusual.

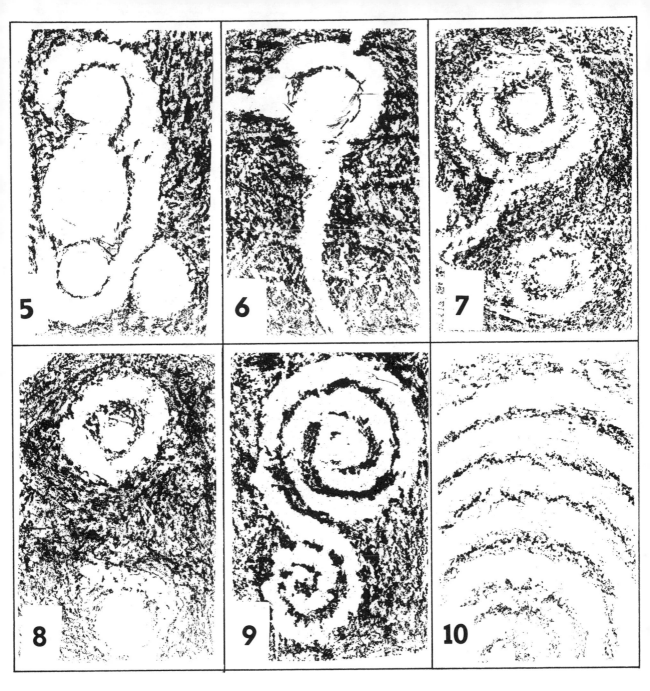

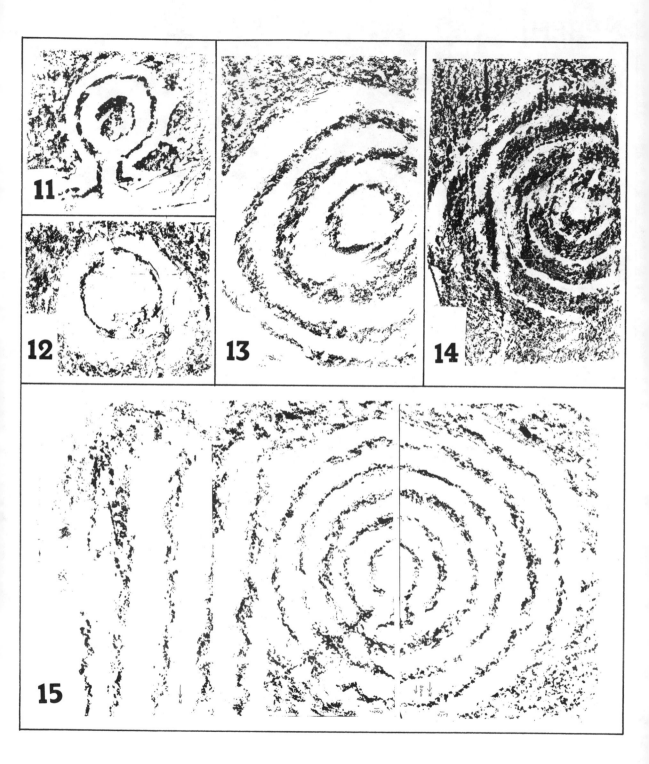

PREHISTORIC ART

The origins and meanings of our prehistoric rock carvings are among the most deeply buried of the great unsolved mysteries in Scotland's and Manx prehistory. At least one hundred and four different theories or hypotheses have been put forward in attempts to explain them.

The carvings have been studied by archaeologists for well over a hundred years. Yet, apart from the careful work of a few men like Sir James Simpson, discoverer of the use of chloroform in anaesthesia, very little has been done to try to classify or analyse them. This book – on the carvings in Galloway, at the extreme South West of Scotland and the neighbouring Isle of Man – is more in the nature of a guide book to their sites than anything else. But it is hoped that it will encourage others to try to discover more about these mysterious carvings in the future.

In my first book, *The Prehistoric Rock Art of Argyll*, I set out to describe and deal with the carved rocks in that district – about eighty of them. As far as possible, in dealing with the hundred and twenty or so sites in Galloway and the Isle of Man, the same pattern has been followed. The area covered here comprises the local government districts of Wigtown and the Stewartry – substantially what was formerly Wigtownshire and the Western part of Kirkcudbrightshire and the Isle of Man. It is hoped, in a final volume, to cover in the same way all the sites in the rest of Southern Scotland, which number around a hundred. There are very few of these old carvings south of Yorkshire or north of Perthshire.

As was the case in *The Prehistoric Rock Art of Argyll*, in addition to the more complex types of carving dealt with in my book, there are about twice as many sites and rocks on which are carved simple cup-marks, and nothing else. Most of these in Galloway are listed in papers I have written in the Proceedings of the Society of Antiquaries of Scotland (P.S.A.S.) and the Transactions of the Ancient Monuments Society (T.A.M.S.) They are omitted here solely because I have felt that, at my time of life (I am over 75), I have too little time left to cover all of them adequately.

As explained in *The Prehistoric Rock Art of Argyll*, it is now possible to give approximate dates for the use of a number of these carvings. This shows that, in Scotland, they were used over a very long period – perhaps from about 3200 BC (cup-marks) to about AD 100 or even later – with a number of 'probable' dates around 1200–1600 BC. In datable cases of use – e.g. cist-slabs – one sometimes can presume that the carving may have been made just before it was put into use. But, clearly, even with cist-slabs, this has not

Some designs, each occurring once only in Galloway.

always been so, and some carvings must have existed long before their final use in such cists. A great many carvings, including practically all on outcrop and all the Manx carvings, are still quite undatable. If you find a cup-and-ring carved on a piece of living, outcropping rock, with no earth now on top of it and absolutely nothing lying around to give any clue whatever, there seems nothing, in our present state of knowledge, to tell you when it was carved. This led, for example, to a carving of a rare spiral at Cockles Smithy in East Lothian being included in the official Inventory of Ancient Monuments of that County, although I found on enquiry that the local blacksmith, a very old man when I saw him, had carved it in his youth as a 'cockle-shell' badge for the Smithy, 'to please my father'.

No matter which of the 'one hundred and four varieties' of theories about these carvings appeals to you, there are several things which are certain:

There was a constant preference for a very small number of 'set' designs in making these, our earliest carvings on rock – the *cup-mark*, which perhaps scarcely is a design in itself, although it can be arranged in rows, rosettes, etc., the *ring*, generally but not always with a *central cup*, and, less often, various forms of *spiral*. Quite often there was a *radial groove* running outwards, and very often downhill, from the central cup, or innermost ring. Sometimes other connecting and non-connecting grooves were also carved. But there was a conspicuous absence in Galloway and the Isle of Man, as in Argyll, of other simple designs, such as zig-zags, triangles, squares, etc., except perhaps on one or two sites.

As I found in Argyll, when they were carved on outcrop rock, the designs were nearly always carved on fairly smooth and nearly horizontal surfaces. Sedimentary rock was usually used, probably because it is easier to carve. The carved outcrops are nearly always situated where they can be seen from quite long distances all around, or – perhaps one should say – where the sun can reach them for most of the day. Copper has been worked and streams have been panned for gold in the past, *only* in the parts of Galloway where these carvings are found, and a little further eastwards. All but two of the carved sites in both Galloway and the Isle of Man lie within 12 kilometres ($7\frac{3}{4}$ miles) of known copper workings, or much nearer than that to gold-bearing streams. Nearly all are within a very few kilometres of the sea. No carving is nearer sea-level than about 12 metres (40 feet) except perhaps **GAL 99**, an Early Christian site included here only for a special reason. Only three sites – **GAL 59, 82** and **83** – are over 330 metres (1000 feet). No carving is in a fortified site. No pottery, tools or bones have been found close to any outcrop site – except, perhaps, in the stone circle near **GAL 61.** Cist-slabs, where carved and where their position in the cist is known, were all carved on their inward-facing side, or left inside the cist. Carvings show up best when the sun at a low angle causes shadows to appear in them, and it is interesting to note that about two-thirds of those carved on sloping outcrops sloped gently north, thus giving better shadow effects in sunshine.

An attempt has been made to classify the material in the Galloway region of southern Scotland into categories, including those mentioned above, and following the pattern I used in *The Prehistoric Rock Art of Argyll.* Forty *elements* have been analysed in the sixteen maps which follow this introduction. It seems inappropriate to comment further here on the Galloway area in isolation. But in the final volume, on the rest of southern Scotland, there will be included a full analysis, with comment, covering the area as a whole.

Armed with this limited knowledge, therefore, let us now consider the one hundred and four theories which have been put forward in all seriousness from time to time by archaeologists and others to explain these mysteries. Besides all listed here, there are probably others which I knew nothing of. I shall be grateful to any reader who will tell me of these and why he (or she) supports them. Many – indeed most – of the theories listed below are still strongly held and believed in by at least one archaeologist of note, amateur or professional.

Some types rather seldom found.

Almost certainly more than one of the theories is correct. In the very long period of the cup-and-ring's use – well over 3000 years in some parts of the British Isles – there was probably more than one use to which the design was put, just as today there is more than one reason for using the Cross, which has been our symbol in Scotland for a mere fifteen hundred years or so. The Cross can, for example, be a Red Cross, a Victoria Cross, a Cross at the head of a grave, or some other variety. Each of these Crosses has a very different meaning. Yet each has, and is derived from, the same central symbolical meaning of Christianity. So it may be with the various uses to which the cup-and-ring and other prehistoric designs were put.

In brackets after each paragraph, I give, with all diffidence, and expecting to be torn to shreds by believers in each theory, my personal assessment of the probability that each idea is correct. '10'

Some common types.

Wilson 1921, p. 45
Scott 1951, p. 69

means that, to me at least, this seems to be a certainty, or nearly so. '5' means that this is a reasonably sensible idea which may or may not be true – I know of nothing either to support it or to contradict it. '0' means that, to me, this seems quite impossible.

Here, then, are the 'one hundred and four varieties' – and several of them are almost certainly correct.

1   BURIALS – slabs bearing these carvings were used in burial ceremonies between about 1600 and 1900 BC, being built into the cist as part of it, carved side usually facing in, or placed loosely inside the cist with the dead body or remains. (10)

2   STANDING STONES – standing stones sometimes bear cup-marks or cups-and-rings. As the carving usually stops about ground level it is held by many that the carvings were made about the date the stone was first erected. Professor A. Thom has suggested that in Argyll this was usually about 2700 to 1500 BC. (9)

3   ALIGNMENT MARKERS – it has been pointed out that in most cases where a standing stone, whether one of a close-knit group or not, is carved, it forms part of an important-seeming alignment on, say, the midwinter sunset, or the point where the moon sets at its most northerly setting point. (10)

4   ASTRONOMY – it is claimed by Professor A. Thom and a growing band of archaeologists that these alignments were very carefully worked out, perhaps over centuries, by the 'wise men', who used them in primitive, but accurate, astronomy – for such things as keeping the dates for sowing correct, for predicting the ebb and flow of the tides and, perhaps, even for predicting lunar and solar eclipses. (9)

5   RE-USE IN BURIAL – quite often cist slabs seem to have been broken through the carving so as to make the panel fit the cist. Also quite often, carvings which have been completely protected from all weather by being faced inwards in the cist are much weathered, as though by action of the elements over a long period, before they were hidden away. It has been suggested that the slabs were merely re-used in the burial. No-one has suggested what that previous use may have been. (9)

6   EARLY PROSPECTORS – many archaeologists have suggested that these carvings were made by the earliest prospectors, searching for copper ores and for gold. In Galloway and the Isle of Man this is supported by the fact that *every carving except two* is within 12 km ($7\frac{3}{4}$ miles) of a place where copper ore has been worked at some time, or is within $1\frac{1}{2}$ km (1 mile) of streams where gold has been panned. Of the two exceptions one – **GAL 51, House**

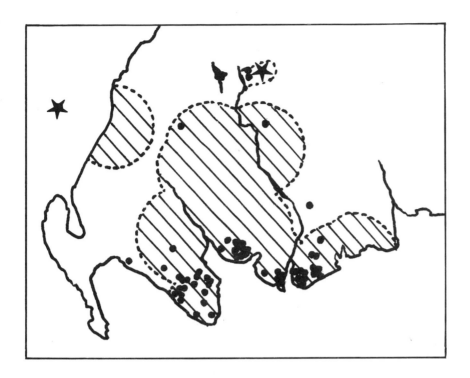

On this map the gold workings are shown starred, a 12-km circle round the copper workings is shaded; and the prehistoric carved sites are all marked. As will be seen, nearly every one of them is near one of these workings, and areas farther from them have no carvings.

of Elrig – is built into a twentieth century house. By the time these early prospectors reached Scotland they must have been well aware what kind of country might yield their ores or metal. 12 km seems a reasonable search area. No mining artifacts, however, have been found near any carved site. (8)

7 EARLY PROSPECTING AIDS – some archaeologists go further and suggest that the carvings were used in some way – magic or religious? – to help to find these metals. (5)

8 BELIEF IN AFTER-LIFE – the fact that, in cists, the great majority (and in fact all in Galloway) are built with a carved slab facing inwards – where there is such a carving – seems to show that the carvers believed this would be of some use to the dead person –

i.e. that in some way the spirit existed after physical death and could still make use of this carved symbol. (8)

9 & 10 RELIGIOUS AND MAGICAL – nearly all the older school of archaeologists, and many today, hold that all this clearly shows that the cup-and-ring and other carvings had a magical or religious significance. (7)

11 & 12 UNIFORM RELIGIOUS OR MAGICAL SIGNIFICANCE – I, and probably many others before me, have suggested that the *same* symbolical magic or religious meaning attached to all of one type of carving, whether used in cists, on standing stones, on outcrop rocks, or otherwise. I have quoted a parallel here with the many uses of the Cross. But we have absolutely no proof. (6)

SEX – a surprising number of theories have been put forward from the time these carvings were first studied right up to the present day – some by very eminent archaeologists such as the Abbé Breuil – based on a sexual interpretation. These include:

Breuil 1934

13 BREASTS – they are drawn to represent the female breast. There are a few examples which seem to support this idea, and many more where, if one isolates two carvings in a group, a photograph of these two supports the theory. With a little imagination these can easily be converted into 'eyes'. (4)

14 MOTHER GODDESS – 'the breasts represent the Mother Goddess. Some other carvings represent in diagrammatic form her fat, distended, figure.' Here, again, one has to exert one's imagination and there is no proof. (4)

15 MOTHER-GODDESS WORSHIP – they were involved in a *ritual* of worshipping this early Goddess, who undoubtedly existed.

Crawford 1957

16 EYES – they represent 'eyes'. An eminent archaeologist has written a book on 'The Eye Goddess'. Again, one has to exert one's imagination and often exclude much of the carved site to see this – e.g. there are two good eyes at least in **GAL 107.** (4)

17 PHALLIC SYMBOLS – some see the symbols, especially the gapped rings with radial groove down the gap, as representing the male sexual organ. Again, one can imagine much. (3)

Grant letter to author, 1978

18 FERTILITY SYMBOLS – '**SPERM ENTERING THE EGG'** – an eminent Californian archaeologist, author of two books on rock art, has recently suggested that 'here we have a fine "graphic" of a wriggling sperm (the radial groove) invading the egg (the rings, to the centre cup).' (2)

19 FERTILITY RITES – in the Hebrides and possibly elsewhere, some cup-marks are still associated with such rites. For example, at a site in the churchyard at Kilchoman in Islay, a pestle is pro-vided, and you turn it in one of the cup-marks on a slab which forms the base of an Early Christian Cross – three times with the sun. You then put a piece of silver in another of the cup-marks. The wish you then make comes true if connected with fertility – e.g. 'may it be a son', 'may we have a good crop' etc. The Church Officer collects the silver periodically and adds it to the church col-lection. It has been suggested that all cup-and-ring carvings were originally made for such fertility rites; but there is no evidence known to me outside Argyll, the Isle of Man and the Hebrides – all cup-marks. (*see also 32 below*) (3)

20 MARKS OF SEXUAL PROWESS – the Chief made a cup-and-ring to celebrate each female conquest he made. (0)

21 CIRCUMCISION CEREMONY – 'hence the phallic sym-bols'. (1)

22 SEX SYMBOLS – of various kinds, with no ulterior meaning. (0)

23 SUN SYMBOL – Continental archaeologists, in Italy and in Scandinavia, for example, have evidence which points to the cup-and-ring having this symbolic meaning; but there is no evidence which supports, or contradicts, this in Britain. (6)

24 SUN GOD – Many on the Continent go farther and claim that the symbol represents the sun *god* – and is a part of sun-worship. There seems no evidence of this in Britain. (5)

25 BAAL – older writers claimed that these symbols were part of the worship of the god Baal; but, again, there is no evidence. (5)

26 WATER DIVINING – to mark the crossing of two under-ground streams. (0)   *Manx source*

27 MIXING VESSELS – for mixing and casting *bronze*, the rings forming overflow channels from which, when cooled, metal strips could be taken for making hooks etc. (2)   *Manx source*

28 MIXING VESSELS – for grinding and blending *pigments* of different colours, one colour being kept in each ring. The author has seen a cup-mark in one of the Faroe Isles which is still used to grind the roots of the tormentil, a small yellow flower, to make a rich brown-yellow dye. (4)   *Manx source*

29 QUANTITY MEASURES – to gauge the quantities of pigments to give a definite colour (e.g. one colour in each ring) or to measure quantities of grain etc, in early trade. (1)   *Manx source*

30 FREEMASONS 'EARLIEST' MARKS – the earliest symbol of the Order – the 'All-seeing Eye'. (0)

31 SACRED FOOD AND WINE HOLDERS – it is said that in

remote parts of Sweden a custom is carried on to this day in which the cup-and-ring carving is used in Spring, for this purpose in an ancient rite. Certainly on the Isle of Seil in Scotland, until less than a century ago, there was a custom in which the youngest dairymaid on the farm had to go up the hill and fill a rather large cupmark with milk each Spring, for the 'wee folk' (fairies). If this was not done, there would be a shortage of milk and food that Autumn. (5)

32   FERTILITY RITES (INDIAN) – In Scandinavia it has been suggested that the true interpretation of their cup-and-ring marks is the same as that in India, where, it is said, the simplest form of the 'yoni' is a cup, representing fire, surrounded by a ring, which may represent the female element, sometimes with a radial groove. Fire was made there by turning a wooden pestel quickly in a cupmark in the rock. The symbol, it is said, unites the two ideas of fire and fertility. (0)

33   COPIES OF WORM CASTS – a leading anthropologist has recently suggested that the carvings may be this, or nos 34 or 35 below. (2)

34   COPIES OF TREE RINGS – see 33 above. (2)

35   COPIES OF RIPPLES FROM A STONE THROWN INTO A POOL – see 33 above. I have seen a beautiful and convincing photograph of such ripple rings in a book on rock art; but have been quite unable to find it again to quote it here. (2)

36   DRUIDS – an older school of archaeologists maintained that the Druids *made* the carvings. The fact that quite a number of sites have such names as 'The Druid Stone' seemed to support this. But, apart from such names, there is no evidence for or against this, nor any evidence as to how old the order of the Druids was before the Romans found them in Britain. (5)

37   USE BY DRUIDS – others maintain that, although not made by the Druids, the Druids continued to *use* the old carvings, perhaps for ceremonies which had been handed down to them by the 'wise men', their predecessors, who had made the carvings, or perhaps for their own, newer, cult, the whole ceremonies being passed down, perhaps for very many generations by word of mouth, perhaps in verse. (5)

38   BLOOD SACRIFICE – it used to be said that Druids or earlier priests used the carvings by filling them with blood from sacrifices and letting the blood run down through the radial grooves and other connecting grooves. In support, it can be said that many sites look like altars, and when one pours water on carvings near the top, it seems to spread fairly evenly over the area of the site as it runs down. But no skeletons, organic remains, or likely pottery or tools, have been found near any outcrop site, so far as known to me, to support this. (4)

39   CODE – Professor A. Thom, very tentatively, and others, have suggested that possibly the carvings, especially those in standing stones, were a code which stored information for the 'wise men' – for example, information, to be used once every nineteen and a half years or so, on astronomical alignments, and calculations from these alignments of coming eclipses. If so, the code has still to be broken. (5)

40   WATER TIME-SIGNALS – it has been suggested that, when filled up with water, they reflect the sun's rays along a known path at exactly the same time each day, so giving a time signal. This certainly is true, but there is no evidence indicating their use in this way. (1)

41   CLOCKS – it has been suggested that they were used (but how?) as sundials, to tell the time of day. (1)

42   PICTOGRAPHS or HIEROGLYPHS – some suggest, without so far attempting to de-code them, that these old carvings were, perhaps the very earliest, attempts at conveying a meaning by a set design. (6)

43   EARLY WRITING – some, with greater imagination, suggest that they are actually an early form of script. (0)

44   MESSAGES FROM OUTER SPACE – some suggest this is what they are – still to be decoded. (0)

45   MEGALITHIC INCH – Having analysed, almost at random, quite a large number of samples of rings and other shapes from rubbings of them submitted to him by me, Professor A. Thom suggests that in Britain a great many (but not all) of these carved rings have a radius which has been measured exactly in megalithic inches (0.816 Imperial Inches) or simple fractions of that inch. (9)

Thom 1968, p. 77

46   ALL MEASURED IN OR FOUNDED ON MEGALITHIC INCHES – some have suggested that this is so. This is quite incorrect. There are some quite irregular rings, which could neither have been measured in, nor founded on, right-angle triangles based on a measurement unit. (0)

Thom 1968, p. 78

47   RIGHT ANGLE TRIANGLES – Professor Thom has further suggested that many non-circles (e.g. ellipses and egg-shapes) are made up from curves based on right-angle triangles laid out in exact megalithic inches or part-inches. This seems true in some cases, but not all. (9)

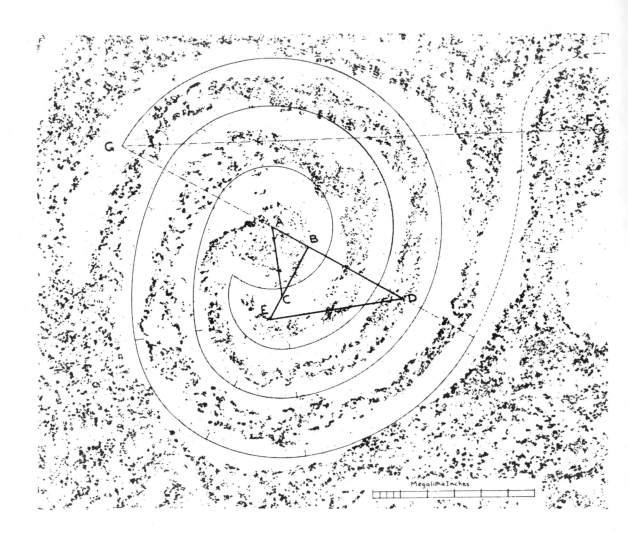

An example of Professor A. Thom's analysis of a spiral carving at Hawthornden, Midlothian. This shows both his use of the right-angle triangles and the megalithic inch (scale on bottom right). The sides of the 2 basic triangles are respectively 5,4, and 3 megalithic inches, and 2½, 2 and 1½ megalithic inches. A 'megalithic inch' is stated by Professor Thom to be 0.816 inches. He points out that the spiral is scribed by making a series of half-circles whose centres are all on one or other of the points A, B, C, D, and E, and he states that, if one starts to look at the spiral at its outer end, G, all the radii are integrated in ¼ megalithic inches until the centre is reached. Coming out from the centre, ½ megalithic inch units have been used. Professor Thom points out that this kind of sequence is only possible when founded on right-angle triangles whose sides have the same unit. The reader will be able to judge for himself how accurately the superimposed semi-circles follow the curves shown in the rubbing. *Reproduced by kind permission of the Ancient Monuments Society.*

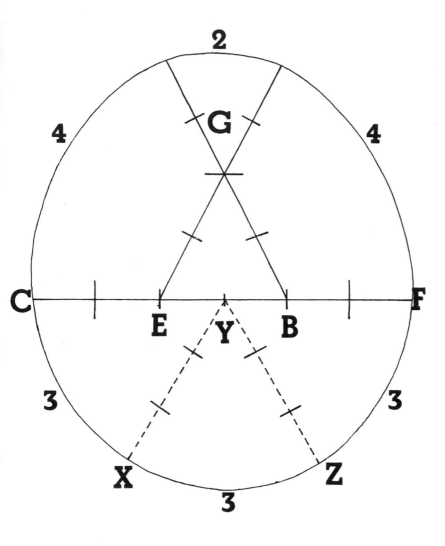

An example of Frau M. Reiche's analysis of an egg-shaped carving at Achnabreck in Argyll **((ARG 3).** This shows how she breaks down all its curves into arcs based on equilateral triangles whose sides have a very simple numerical relationship to each other. Unfortunately, none of the examples of her work in the author's hands have been superimposed on rubbings, as in most cases she made the drawing by tracing directly from the carving concerned, on the site. Here, the sides of the triangles are of 4, 3, and 2 units. She suggests that the same unit was used throughout any one site, but that it may vary slightly between one site and another, perhaps being based on a part of the body, say, a thumb-joint.

Thom 1968, p. 78

48 EQUILATERAL TRIANGLES – Frau Maria Reiche, who has spent over 30 years studying the Nasca lines in Peru, on the evidence of a few random samples of rubbings of some Scottish ellipses and other non-circles, has tentatively claimed that, like her Nasca drawings, all those she tested were based on the curves between the two points of a series of equilateral triangles whose sides have a very simple ratio in length to each other, the same unit of measurement having been used for all the carvings *on the one site*. At the time of writing, she has asked for more examples in the hope that she can prove her theory applies to all sites. (6)

49 CODE – she further suggests that the number of units of length used in each of her equilateral triangles, when used together for a site as a whole, may give a code used by the 'wise men' when working with the sites. She has not suggested how this might be interpreted. (1)

50 SPIRALS ARE TWO-CENTRE HALF-CIRCLES OR ELLIPSES – Professor Thom has shown that every set of rubbings of every Scottish spiral so far submitted to him was composed of a series of half-circles (or half-ellipses). Using two sets of centres, the circle's radius (or the sides of the right-angle triangle on which the ellipse was based) were increased by a fixed amount of megalithic half-inches as the spiral proceeded outwards. This evidence seems to me to be the most conclusive and convincing I have so far seen of the existence of the megalithic inch. (7)

51 DIFFERENT RACES MADE THEM – some leading archaeologists distinguish two entirely different sets of these carvings – on the one hand spirals, rings without central cups and a few other forms rarely found in south-west Scotland; on the other hand cups-and-rings. Cup-marks are places in both categories. It is said that the first category, mostly found in passage graves (mostly in Ireland) and called the 'Boyne type', were made by one race, while the cup-and-ring type were made by another race, possibly from Galicia in north-west Iberia. These they call 'Galician'. There is clearly some overlap between the two types. While this is an attractive theory, there is no actual concrete evidence to support it, except the siting of the carvings – cups-and-rings mostly on outcrops and 'Boyne-types' mostly in tombs. (7)

52 BONFIRE RITUAL SITE MARKERS – in Switzerland such cup-and-ring carvings are sometimes found associated with bonfire sites of very old standing, and indeed this is the case with a cup-marked site on a hill in Tiree, Argyll. A Swiss archaeologist has suggested that these outcrop carvings, both here and in Switzerland, nearly all on open sites visible from all around, were all associated with bonfire-lighting ceremonies. (6)

53 SEARCH FOR FOOD – at least one archaeologist has suggested that the carvings were placed where they are in course of some form of search for food. (2)

54 SEED PRODUCTION – it has also been suggested that they were carved in some way to aid in seed production. (1)

55 EARLY PILGRIMAGE MARKS – the late Earl of Cawdor has seen pilgrims in Tibet making cup-marks on their way to, and on reaching, a Holy Place. But there is no evidence to support any such use here. (1)

56 DYE-TRANSFER MOULDS – in actual experiments, an archaeologist has shown that it is possible to get quite an attractive pattern on a skin by spreading it over a carved site after filling the carvings with dye. This would, he points out, account for the sites nearly all being roughly horizontal. (6)

57 METAL MOULDS – but how? (0)

58 MAPS OF THE COUNTRYSIDE – perhaps one or two – especially in Northumberland – resemble maps; but I very much doubt if this is more than a coincidence. (1)

59 BUILDING PLANS – (e.g. of a hill fort) – again perhaps one or two, especially in Northumberland, look rather like this; but no such resemblance can be seen in the sites in Galloway. (0)

60 STAR MAPS – archaeologists on both sides of the border and abroad have tried to show that this is what the carvings are laid out to show. Especially if one ignores all the carvings which do not fit one's ideas, one can quite often make out a simple constellation like 'the Plough' or *ursa major* on a carved site. But I doubt if this, too is anything but coincidence and wishful thinking. (1)

61 'EMBLEMS' – of the Druids, clans, or 'wise men' of bygone ages. (5)

62 TATTOOISTS' PATTERNS – we know tattooing existed among the Celts when the Romans first recorded these things. It is suggested that it had been in use in far earlier times on these islands and that, possibly painted in colour, these cups-and-rings and others were the tattooists' very effective 'shop window'. If one tries this by colouring in the carvings on a site with coloured chalk, the result is certainly marvellous – and very photogenic! (5)

63 DECORATIONS – it is argued by some that the carvings had no significance, but were intended for simple decoration of the rock or slab. Quite possibly this may have been one of the uses to which some carvings were put. But arguments can be put forward against *ALL* of them being merely decor. Why decorate the *inside* of a tomb-slab, for example? (5)

64 DOODLES – not even decoration, just done by someone who had time to spare. (2)

65 AN ELDERLY MAN'S 'SCREEN' – while the young were out hunting and the women working in the field, the old men of the 'clan' carved these designs, so that, on the young's return, they could pretend they had all sorts of magic, and so impress the young. But really the old men knew they meant very little. (2)

66 BOUNDARY MARKERS – perhaps of a family's territory. But, if this was so, the land must have been divided in a very strange way. (1)

67 ROUTE MARKERS – in the days before tracks or roads, they were made to mark the way for early traders and travellers. (5)

68 TRIBAL CONVENTION COMMEMORATORS – made to commemorate some outstanding tribal meeting or the like. (3)

69 MITHRAS WORSHIP – made in Roman times, and used in the worship of their god, Mithras. The dating available does not support this. (0)

70 SHIELDS – they represent shields, which in early times were circular. (0)

71 GAMING TABLES – they were used for a kind of hoop-la. Certainly in Malta there is a fairly large rock slab with about 16 cup-marks in it, which is said to have been used for this purpose, and for which some of the gaming accessories have been found. But there is no supporting evidence for this use (or against it) on any site known to me in Britain. (3)

72 MARBLES – they were used for an early form of a game with marbles. But why have we found no marbles? (3)

73 ANNULAR BROOCHES – they were patterns for making annular brooches, or represent sales patterns used by vendors of these. No evidence. No brooches found nearby. (3)

74 ANIMISTIC CARVINGS – in a much wider sense – representing many parts of the body, or animals. If one looks at a big assemblage of these carvings long enough, one can imagine almost anything. (0)

75 PRIMITIVE LAMP BASES – to hold oil and a wick. (0)

76 WATER WORSHIP – stone images of what happens on throwing a pebble into a pool, water being the god. (5)

77 CATTLE WORSHIP – the cow is sacred in the East – images of its cow-pats. (2)

78 MARKS OF PIETY – made on a Holy *rock*, according to a religious creed – the *rock*, not the mark, being the Holy object. (5)

79 RE-USE OF A LONG DEAD SUPERSTITION – e.g. when such cup-and-ring carvings are found in crannogs or souterrains. Possibly the users did not know exactly what they were, but knew they were used in a superstitious way by their ancestors – like our Christmas tree, perhaps. (5)

80 MONUMENTS TO THE DEAD – *ALL*, including outcrop carvings, represent a memorial to some long-dead person of note. (1)

81 NATURAL – *ALL* are entirely the results of weathering and unusual naturally-occurring rock shapes and strata. (0)

82 HIDDEN TREASURE – they are secret plans to show where this was hidden. (0)

83 PLANS FOR MEGALITHIC STRUCTURES – (0)

84 PLANS FOR LAYING OUT MAZES – on the ground nearby. (0)

85 FIELD PLOUGHING PLANS – (0)

86 OATH MARKS – for example, oaths of fealty might have been taken by inscribing the rock in this way, for all to see. (5)

87 VICTORY MARKS – each one was made by the local chief to celebrate a victory over an adjoining tribe. (1)

88 MASONS' MARKS – perhaps the earliest form of these. (0)

89 ADDER LAIRS – entirely the result of countless generations of adders coiling over the rock in a certain way, and wearing these marks in it. (0)

90 KNIFE-SHARPENING MARKS – caused by use over a very long period for sharpening knives and other tools. (0)

91 AN EARLY FORM OF MUSIC NOTATION – (0)

92 TUNING DEVICE – by carving them the 'wise men' could alter the pitch of any rock's natural vibration to the pitch desired, so that it would ring true to tone, as does the cup-marked 'ringing stone' on Tiree. But does any other stone or outcrop ring? (0)

93 EARLY ASTRONOMER'S NIGHT MEMORANDA – working over the indentations on a dark night, perhaps in time with an age-old verse, and moving the hand, by feeling, from one indentation to another as certain celestial events occurred in the night, perhaps of the new moon, the 'wise men" were enabled to know when the looked-for rising might be expected to occur. (2)

94 BIRTH, GROWTH, LIFE AND DEATH SYMBOL – a leading amateur archaeologist has suggested that they were intended to include in the one symbol all these four human elements. (5)

95 A LOCKED-UP FORCE – laser-beam holograms sometimes look very like cup-and-ring marks. This has caused some 'fringe' archaeologists to suggest that, if only we knew the code and could un-leash this mighty Force, perhaps by use of neighbouring stone circles, ley lines, or standing stones, we could control the universe. (0)

96 THE STONE CIRCLE BUILDERS CARVED THEM – Professor Thom writes – 'since the unit of measurement used (e.g. in carving a spiral) is *exactly* one fortieth of the Megalithic yard (used in erecting stone circles), and since the conventions are identical with those governing the design of the stone circles of the Megalithic peoples, the conclusion is inescapable that the latter (i.e. the Megalithic peoples) were also responsible for the cup-and-ring'. (8)

Thom 1968, p. 81

97 HEALING MAGIC – if a sick person were to go round the stones three times in a sun-wise direction he might be cured of a specific ailment'. But there is no evidence for or against this. (5)

98 CASTS FOR MAKING BRONZE – the 20% tin (imported) and 80% copper (local) were put respectively into the cups and into the surrounding rings. The 'tail', if any, carried away the dross downhill. But how was heat applied? And why are there no metal remains, or dross remains, at any site? (3)

99 The carvings, very often broken off or worn, found on the faces of stone cists, represent the 'tools' of, or used in some way by, the person buried there – like stone axes and other artifacts so found. (6)

100 SEA GODDESS WORSHIP – the cup, or cup-and-rings represents a mirror, and the radial groove the handle. Filled with water, light and images are reflected – c.f. the ancient mermaid drawn with a mirror – all as worship to the Sea Goddess. (1)

101 MIRROR – whether or not they represent the Sea Goddess, the carvings represent a mirror and its handle. There is no evidence against this. (5)

102 WOMB SYMBOL – the cup, filling with water, and draining again, is the womb (is the ring the woman?). The radial groove is the baby's neck, or the birth passage. There is no evidence against this. (5)

103 WELLS – the carvings were placed so as to mark these, perhaps healing wells. (0)

104 CHILD CARVINGS – just as the vandals of today paint on walls etc., so the children of ancient times carved these carvings, without any special significance. (0)

Well, these are some of the theories about these old carvings.

Now for the facts:

In what follows I have listed the sites in Galloway and in the Isle of Man in alphabetical order under the names – mostly the farm names – used in any previous paper about them. Sites which are nearer each other than 25 metres usually have not been given separate numbers, even if they were listed separately in earlier papers. In some farms, such as Cairnholy, earlier papers included cup-marked rocks and each site was given a consecutive number – e.g. *Cairnholy 4*. In these cases I have kept the old number for the farm site, and as a result – because of the omission of sites bearing cup-marks only – the numbers used may not be consecutive. Also, after the original manuscript and maps had been prepared, one or two additional sites were discovered, and one or two were deleted from the list for one reason or another – again causing the numbers not always to be consecutive, or to have an extra number such as '12A' included.

At the end of the book you will find an alphabetical list of some other names by which some of the sites have been known or referred to. The bibliography at the end of the book explains the abbreviations used in referring to earlier papers about each site in the margins.

You will find that I have stated at the beginning of what is written about each site: where it is, its National Grid map reference, height above sea-level, and on which Ordnance Survey map it appears. At the date of going to press Ordnance Survey maps are gradually being changed over to a new series based on metres and this may take a number of years. So, in each case, both the old and the new sheet numbers for both the one-inch and the six-inch series of maps and their approximate new equivalents are given. For a similar reason, nearly all measurements are given both in Imperial and in Metric measurements.

I am indebted to the Archaeology Division of the Ordnance Survey for giving me nearly all the eight-figure references which appear for many sites in the text. In searching for such small, inconspicuous objects as these carvings, to have a map reference to within ten metres, as opposed to the hundred metres of accuracy for the more usual six-figure reference, is a very real help. The Division has also given me much other help, including the checking of nearly all the map numbers and grid references given in the text. Where a six-figure reference is given, it is my own estimate of the position of a site as yet not examined by the Ordnance Survey. The map references are not always *completely* accurate, but they will be found to be very nearly correct. The new maps are really excellent, and the larger-scale maps can be of real help in locating a hard-to-find site.

Every site listed in the book has been visited by me at least once. Many of them have been visited much more often than that - some perhaps a dozen times. Nearly all are hard to photograph, and one must have a really *low* sun on a wet rock surface for best results – a combination not always easy to find, or to forecast, when living a hundred miles away from this lovely country of Galloway, and further still from the fair Isle of Man.

The scales which appear in many of the photographs are always divided into 5 cm black-and-white sections, unless otherwise stated in the caption. All the photographs and diagrams, maps etc., are my own unless I have stated otherwise. All diagrams of carvings are to scale 3 : 100, unless otherwise stated.

You will find a list of easily accessible sites at the end of this book. If you have not seen them already, you may care to visit these first. Looking at these and some of the other sites covered in the book may at least help you to decide which of the theories listed above is *not* likely to be the true explanation of the cup-and-ring's mysterious origin.

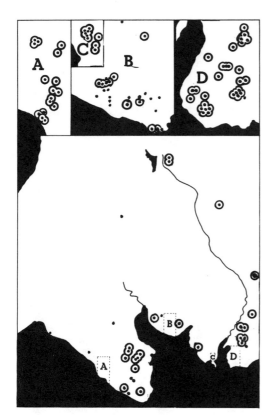

Carvings on outcrop rock.

Carvings on big, immoveable, boulders.

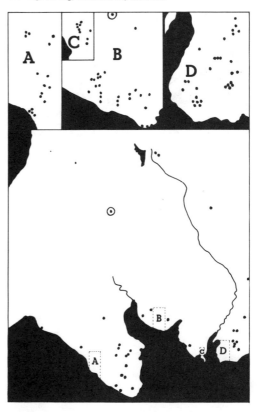

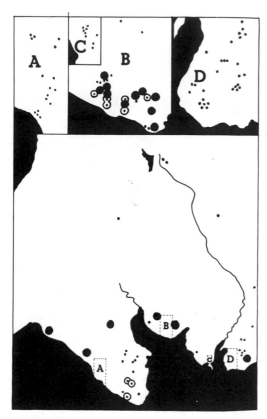

Carvings on smaller, movable, boulders:— ● fairly large ones. ⊚ small, portable, ones.

Carvings on cist-slabs, or possible cist slabs:— ● on one side only. ▲ on both sides. ⊙ on possible cist slabs (no cist found).

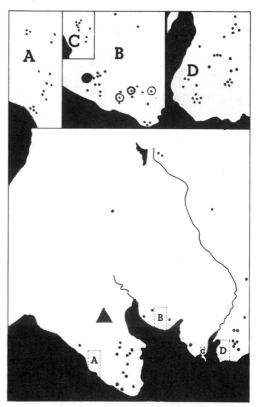

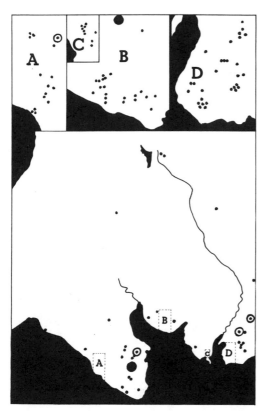

Carvings of spirals:— ● Existing spirals. ◉ Spirals formerly reported, not now found.

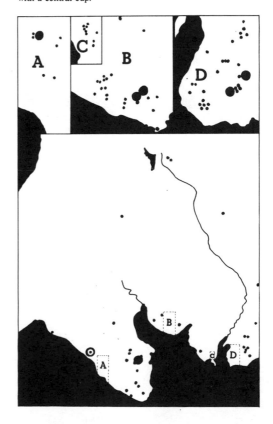

"Keyhole-type" carvings:— ◉ with no central cup. ● with a central cup.

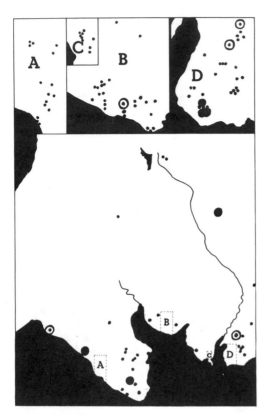

Carvings of rings with no central cup:— ● alone. ◉ with other cups-and-rings.

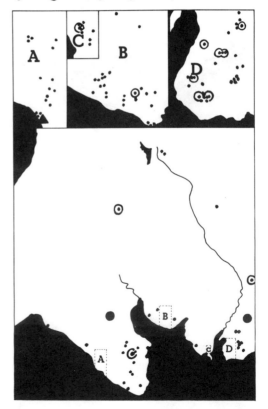

Other Carvings:— ● including "rays". ▲ including "grids". ◉ including other geometric patterns.

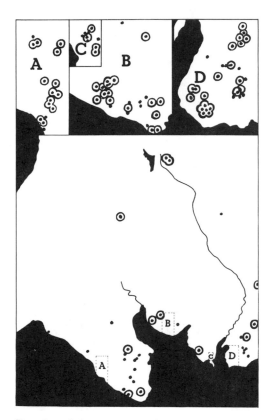

Sites where all rings are un-gapped.

Sites where both gapped and un-gapped rings occur on same stone (**note** — in some cases apparent gaps may just represent weathering off).

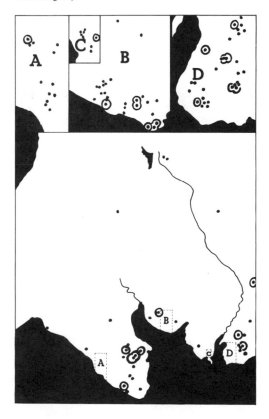

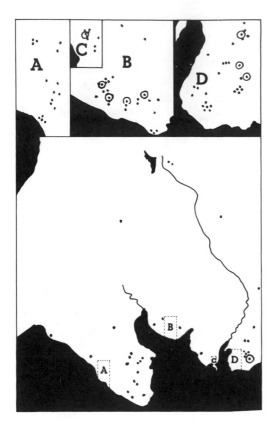

Sites where all rings are gapped or incomplete.

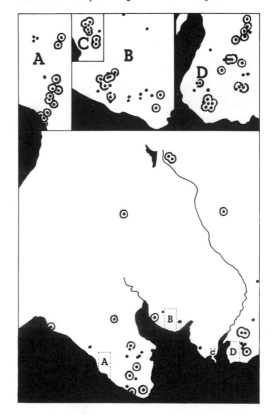

Sites where no cup-and-ring contains a radial groove.

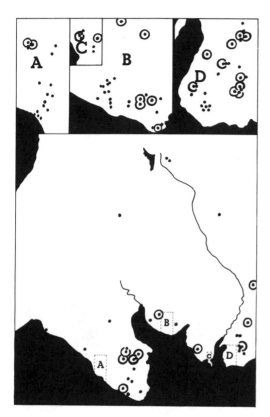

Sites where some cups-and-rings have radial grooves and others have none.

Sites where some of the radial grooves run from the cup and some from the ring only.

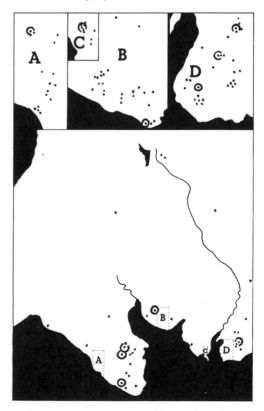

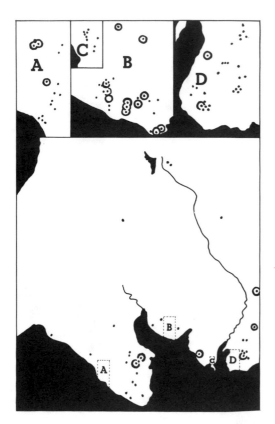

Sites where all radial grooves found run from the cup at centre.

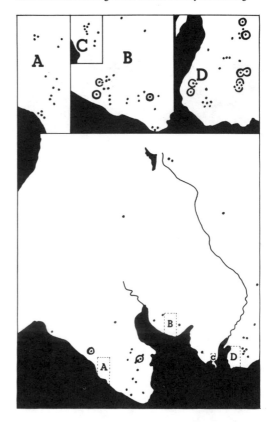

Sites where all radial grooves found run only from a ring.

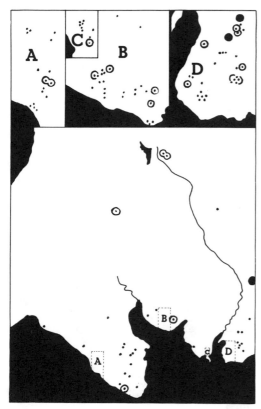

Sites where the maximum is one ring:— ⊙ with central cup, in all cases. ● ring only, alone.

Sites where the maximum is 2 rings:— ⊙ with central cup, in all cases. ● rings only, in some cases.

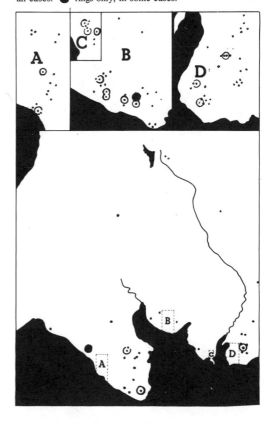

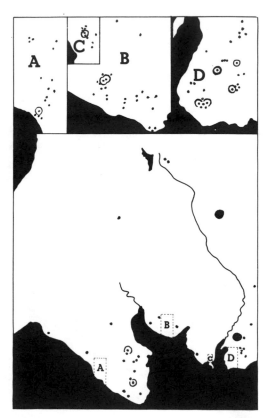

Sites with maximum 3 rings:— ⊚ with central cup, in all cases. ● rings only, in some cases.

Sites with maximum 4 or more rings:— ⊙ all with central cup. ● some with rings only.

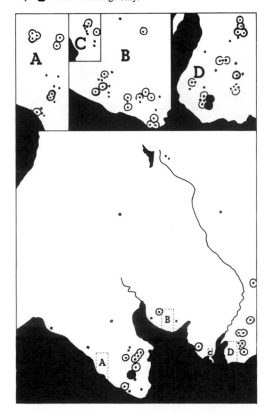

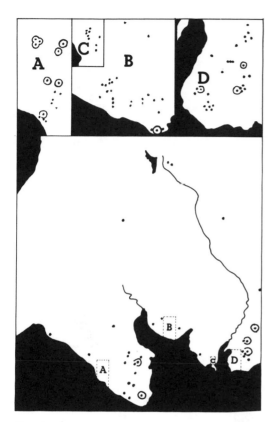

Carved surfaces mostly sloping N.W. to N.N.E.

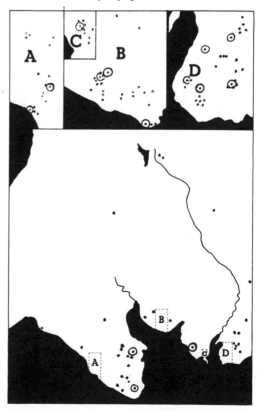

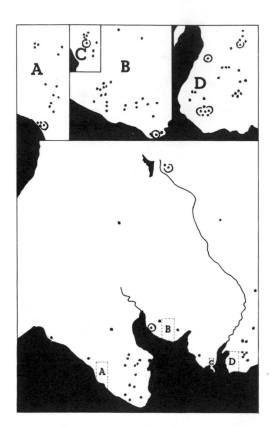

Carved surfaces mostly sloping S.W. to W.N.W.

Carved surfaces mostly sloping S.E. to S.S.W.

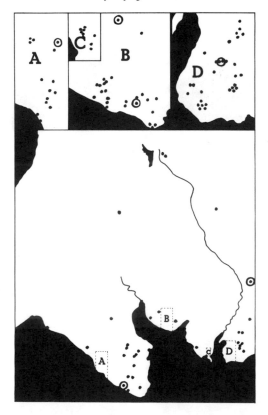

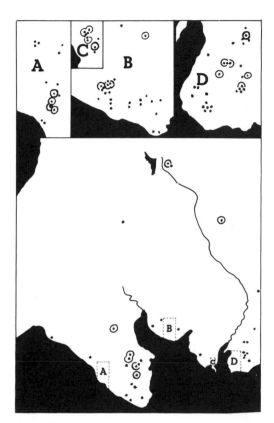

All carvings on nearly horizontal rock.

Carved surfaces mostly at an angle to horizontal between 0° and 25° approximately.

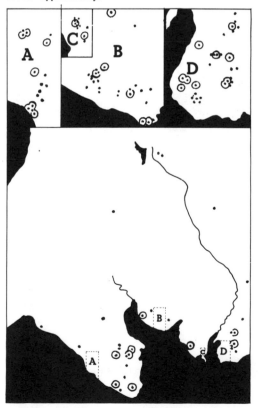

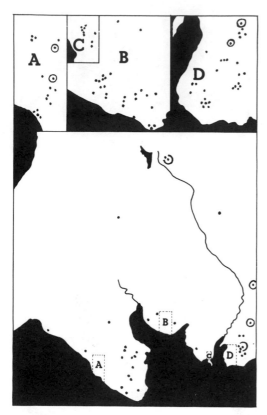

Carved surfaces mostly at an angle between 25° and 45° to horizontal.

The sites in relation to mineral workings. The area within hatched lines is within 12 km (7¾ miles) of a place where copper or its ore is known to have been worked at some time. ▨ — a possible "search" area. The dotted area in the north is roughly where gold has been searched for in streams at some time.

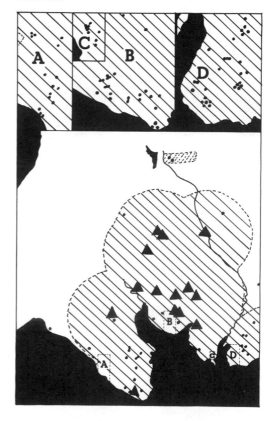

CATALOGUE OF SITES

BALCRAIG 1

Coles 1898, p. 370
 ('Balcroy')
McWhite 1946, p. 80
Morris & Bailey 1964,
 p. 169
Morris 1966, p. 82 &
 102

Outcrop sheets 600 m NW of farm ('Big Balcraig' on some maps). 4 km ENE of Port William and inland, open inland views all round, in grass (former moor). First reported by F. R. Coles (1898).

NX 377 444 OS: old 80 and Wigtownshire 31 NW; new 83 and NX 34 SE. 50 m (160 ft).

(1a) In the Scottish Development Department's care, in a fenced enclosure 27 m (30 yds) S of Far New England Field's N wall, 63 m (70 yds) E of its W wall, is a smooth greywacke outcrop, mostly sloping 25° NW, about 6 m by $4\frac{1}{2}$ m at ground level (20 ft × 14 ft), partly split by turf. On it are –

5 cups-and-complete-rings, having respective 9, 7, 6, 5 and 1 rings, up to 76 cm (30 in) diameters and $\frac{1}{2}$ cm ($\frac{1}{4}$ in) deep, 5 broken-off concentric rings ('arches') and 2 cups. A one-convolution spiral was formerly noted here, as shown dotted on the plan, but the author has never been able to trace this. The carvings are much weathered.

(1b) 11 m (12 yds) NNW of the above enclosure the author in 1977 noticed a long rough greywacke outcrop, 9 m by $3\frac{1}{2}$ m (30 ft × 12 ft) curving S with the ground from horizontal to near-vertical, all at ground level. On a striated central part, sloping about 30°S is – a much-weathered cup-and-three-complete-rings, diameter 30 cm by 26 cm, up to $\frac{1}{2}$ cm deep (12 in × $10\frac{1}{2}$ in × $\frac{1}{4}$ in). There are also about 90 probably natural hollows up to 10 cm by 7 cm, 2 cm deep (4 in × 3 in × $\frac{3}{4}$ in)

BALCRAIG 1A — looking S.E. in the New England field. As in all the pictures, the measure, or hanging rod, shows 5 cm divisions in black.

BALCRAIG 1 A — the two Northmost carvings, looking S. The one on the right has nine rings, the greatest number found in Scotland.

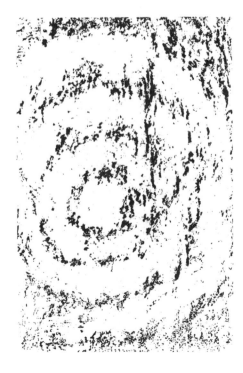

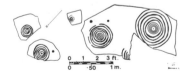

Above: BALCRAIG 1A — Scale 1/75th. The spiral shown in dotted lines — seen in 1898 — seems now to have weathered off.
Left: BALCRAIG 1B — a rubbing of this cup-and-ring carving, first noticed by the author in 1978.

47

W. Inventory 1912, no.
16

Morris & Bailey 1964,
p. 169
Morris 1966, p. 102

Outcrop sheet, 600 m W of farm, 4 km ENE of Port William and sea, in similar situation as GAL 1. First reported by the Royal Commission on Ancient Monuments of Scotland (1912).

NX 373 440 OS: old 80 and Wigtownshire 35 NE; new 83 and NX 34 SE. 50 m (160 ft).

In the Scottish Development Department's care, in a fenced enclosure in Near Windlestraw field, about 120 m (130 yds) N of road B7021, 270 m (300 yds) E of a wood, is a greywacke outcrop mostly sloping 15°N where carved, 6 m by 5 m (20 ft × 16 ft), up to $\frac{1}{3}$ m (1 ft) high. On it are –

    10 cups-and-complete-rings, from 1 to 9 rings, and up to 75 cm (29 in) diameters, also 1 cup. Greatest carving depth 1 cm ($\frac{1}{2}$ in). Much weathered.

BALCRAIG 2 — a big carving.

BALCRAIG 2 — the group in its enclosure, looking S.

Right: BALCRAIG 2 — scale 1/75th.

BALMAE 1

Outcrop sheet 450 m W of Little Balmae farmhouse, $6\frac{1}{4}$ km S of Kirkcudbright, $\frac{3}{4}$ km inland, in rough grass, wide views (sea from near). First reported by G. Hamilton (1886).

Hamilton 1886, p. 156, no. 10
Coles 1894, p. 68, fig. 5
Morris & Bailey 1964, p. 165
K. Inventory 1914, no. 246, fig. 96
Morris 1966, p. 102.

NX 6864 4469 OS: old 80 and Kirkcudbright 58 NW; new 83 and NX 64 SE. 45 m (140 ft).

BALMAE 1 — looking N.N.E. towards the corner of Balmae House's garden wall. The ranging rod is on the site.

On the Army's Heavy Weapons Practice Range (permission must be had before any visit), 115 m (125 yds) SSW of the NE corner of former Balmae House's garden wall, in very rough ground (possibly result of army shelling), is a greywacke horizontal outcrop $1\frac{3}{4}$ m by $1\frac{1}{2}$ m and up to $\frac{1}{4}$ m high (6 ft × 5 ft × $\frac{3}{4}$ ft). On it are –

2 much-weathered irregular un-gapped concentric ovals 70 cm by 53 cm (28 in × 21 in), surrounding 2, and possibly 3, cups, and a short groove, also 5 other cups. Greatest carving depth – 1 cm ($\frac{1}{2}$ in). ARMY PERMISSION MUST BE OBTAINED BEFORE VISITING THIS SITE.

BALMAE 1 — The carvings, looking S.S.W.

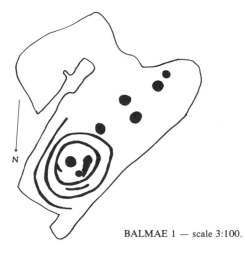

BALMAE 1 — scale 3:100.

In the same area of Army Heavy Weapons Practice Range, also in very rough, much-shelled, ground, were at least seven other similar outcrop cup-and-ring-carved stones, none of which is now traceable. All were first reported by G. Hamilton and F. R. Coles (1886–1894).

K. Inventory 1914, no. 246
Morris & Bailey 1964, p. 165

Morris 1966, p. 102

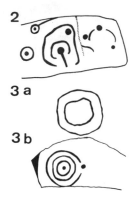

Scale 3:100.

Coles, 1894, pp. 68–71, fig. 4

BALMAE 2 – some 30 ft (9 m) W of Balmae 1, according to the Royal Commission on Ancient Monuments of Scotland (1911) (or 5 m NE, according to Mr. D. C. Bailey in 1965), an outcrop had –

An irregular gapped cup-and-two-rings, 43 cm by 30 cm (17 in × 12 in), with a radial groove from the cup and a second cup within the outer ring, also 2 other cups-and-one-complete ring, 3 cup-marks, and some grooves.

In 1973, at the site indicated by Mr. Bailey, only faint cup-marks could be traced. Coles noted that this site was 'a few yards (m) from Ross View Cottage'. While the cottage no longer exists, this may help to 'fix' the site of Balmae 3 (below).

Coles 1894, p. 68–71 & fig. 1
Hamilton 1886, p. 156 & no. 8

Coles 1894, pp. 68–71 & fig. 2
Hamilton 1886, p. 156 & no. 9

BALMAE 3 – (a) about 100 yds (90 m) S of the now non-existent Ross View Cottage (see above) and probably about 400 m (438 yds) W of Little Balmae farmhouse, on a W-sloping outcrop were –

2 ill-formed concentric rings, up to 43 cm (17 in) diameter, with no cup-marks.

(b) A few yards (m) N of this, on a small rock, were –

A cup-and-three-complete-rings 33 cm (13 in) diameter, with a cup in its outer ring.

In 1965, searching for these, Mr. D. C. Bailey found only a cup-and-one-ring, on an outcrop 90 m (100 yds) SSW of the NE corner of Balmae House's garden wall. But by 1973 only the cup remained un-weathered off.

BALMAE 4 – On an unspecified site in this area Coles also noted –
2 overlapping cups-and-two-complete-rings 33 cm (13 in) diameters.

*Coles 1894, pp. 68–71 &
fig. 3*
*Hamilton 1886, p. 156
& no. 9*

BALMAE 5 – Some 300 yds (270 m) SE of Balmae House (now in ruins) Coles noted, on W-sloping outcrops –

(a) A cup-and-five-complete-rings 60 cm (24 in) diameter and also 4 concentric rings with no cup, and

*Coles 1894, pp. 68–71 &
fig. 5*

(b) Immediately below this – 5 concentric rings 46 cm (18 in) diameter, no cup.

Coles 1894, p. 71

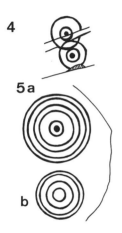

Scale 3:100.

BALMAE 6 – To the N of Balmae House (ruins) on the home field Coles noted a cup-and-part-ring 18 cm (7 in) diameter, which was thirteen inches (33 cm) from the upper, NE, corner of the rock.

Coles 1894, p. 71
*Coles' Sketches sheet
VI(3)*

BALMAE 7 – In his sheets of drawings deposited with the Kirkcudbright Museum, Coles has also sketched another set of 4 concentric rings, diameter 46 cm (18 in) but gives no location details on the estate.

*Coles' Sketches sheet
VII(3)*

There are other cup-marked outcrops in this area. ARMY PERMISSION MUST BE OBTAINED BEFORE VISITING ANY OF THESE BALMAE SITES AS PRACTICE SHELLING IS STILL CARRIED OUT.

Slab found on the farm 'among the stones of an old drain', now missing – about 8 km SW of Gatehouse-of-Fleet. First reported by F. R. Coles (1894).

NX 53 53 OS: old 80 and Kirkcudbright 47 SE; new 83 and NX 55 SW.

Coles 1894 p. 90
Truckell 1961, p. 192
K. Inventory 1914, no. 19
Morris & Bailey 1964, p. 161
Morris 1966, p. 102

Coles' sketch shows a slab like a cist-cover, giving no dimensions. On it are–
    2 cups-and-two-rings, one incomplete, the other with complete rings and radial groove from the cup, 4 gapped-cups-and-one-ring and 4 cups. Many of these figures are connected by grooves.

BARDRISTANE 2

Small slab, found somewhere on the farm, now held by Mrs. Rae, at 17 Merse Road, Kirkcudbright. Cast in the National Museum of Antiquities, Edinburgh no. IA 43. First reported by D. P. Maclagan (1937).

Maclagan 1937, p. 14

NX 53 53 0S: same as GAL 10.

Greywacke slab 30 cm by 20 cm, 4 cm thick (12 in × 8 in × 1¼ in). On its smooth, flat, face is –

A cup-and-four-gapped-rings, the fourth incomplete, 15 cm (6 in) diameter, with radial groove from its cup extending 10 cm (4 in) to end in a second cup.

BARDRISTANE 2 — now held by Mrs. Rae, 17 Merse Road, Kirkcudbright.

GAL 12

BARHOLM 1

Maclagan 1933, p. 414
Morris & Bailey 1964,
  p. 161
Morris 1966, p. 102.

Small slab found somewhere on Barholm Hill, now at Kirkdale House (NX 515 533), originally 8 km WSW of Gatehouse-of-Fleet, about 2 km inland, on moor. Cast no IA 40 in National Museum of Antiquities, Edinburgh. First reported by D. P. Maclagan (1933).

NX 53 55 OS: old 80 and Kirkcudbright 47 SE; new 83 and NX 55 NW.

Smooth flat greywacke slab $\frac{1}{2}$ m by $\frac{1}{3}$ m by 10 cm (2 ft × 1 ft × 4 in). On it are –

A cup-and-two-gapped-rings, 16 cm (6 in) diameter, with a radial groove from the cup extending to the slab's edge. Greatest depth of carving 2 cm (1 in).

BARHOLM 1 — now in the garden shed at Kirkdale House, Anwoth.

BARHOLM 2

GAL 12a

Rectangular block, now in a wall 6 m SE of farm, 9 km WSW of Gatehouse-of Fleet, ½ km inland, wide sea views, in pasture. First reported by I. F. Macleod (1969).

McLeod 1969, p. 28

NX 5206 5299 OS: old 80 and Kirkcudbright 47 SE; new 83 and NX 55 SW. 100 m (320 ft).

6 m (6½ yds) SE of steading's SE corner, built in as the third cornerstone from the foot of the garden wall, is a greywacke block ¾ m by ½ m by ⅓ m (2½ ft × 1½ ft × 1 ft). On its smooth E face are –

A cup-and-two-complete-rings 14 cm (5½ in) diameter, the outer ring, however, 'ballooning' out to enclose a second cup, also a cup-and-one-complete-ring and at least 1 cup. Greatest carving depth ½ cm (¼ in).

It has been reported to the author that the former occupier of the farm knew of another cup-and-ring carving 'somewhere on the farm', but as far as the author knows, this has not yet been traced for noting.

BARHOLM 2 — at present built into the farm's garden wall.

GAL 13 BLACKHILL COTTAGE

Coles 1894, pp. 75–76
K. Inventory 1914, no.
    245.
Morris & Bailey 1964,
    p. 165.
Morris 1966, p. 104.

Outcrop 'lump' 73 m ESE of the cottage, 4½ km S of Kirkcudbright, 1½ km inland, wide views inland, on moor. First reported by F. R. Coles (1894).

NX 6933 4663 OS: old 80 and Kirkcudbright 55 SW; new 83 and NX 64 NE. 90 m (300 ft).

The cottage is about 220 m (240 yds) E of Grange–Townhead road. Although it is 1 m by ¾ m and ¼ m high on its N (3 ft × 2 ft × 9 in), nearly horizontal but domed, this greywacke lump is hard to find among others. On it are –

3 cups-and-rings, with one, two, and three rings respectively, up to 21 cm (8½ in) diameter, 2 sets complete, one broken off at the edge, a basin 15 cm (6 in) diameter, and at least 9 cups. Greatest carving depth 2 cm (1 in). In 1911 it was reported that all rings were complete, and there was a fourth cup-and-one-ring.

BLACKHILL COTTAGE — the carvings, looking S.E.

BLACKHILL COTTAGE — the ring shown in dotted lines has now weathered off.

BLACKHILL COTTAGE — the stone, looking south.

BLACKMYRE

Slab found in a wall on the farm, about 3 km SE of Creetown, 2 km inland, now in the Museum, Kirkcudbright. First reported by J. Flett (1926).

Flett 1926, pp. 140–143
Morris & Bailey 1964,
* p. 161.*
Morris 1966, p. 104.

NX 497 570 OS: old 80 and Kirkcudbright 47 NW; new 83 and NX 45 NE. 155 m (500 ft).

On rebuilding the wall between Long Field and Old Meadow, near its centre, there was found a flat roughly rectangular sandstone slab, perhaps once part of a cist, 56 cm by 43 cm by 23 cm ($1\frac{3}{4}$ ft × $1\frac{1}{2}$ ft × $\frac{3}{4}$ ft). On it are –

10 much-weathered cups-and-rings, having from 1 to 4 rings and up to 20 cm (8 in) diameters, some rings complete, others gapped, some with a radial groove from the cup, and one being an oval cup with oval ring round it. There are also some connecting grooves.

BLACKMYRE — the slab, now in the Kirkcudbright museum.

BLAIRBUY 1

W. Inventory 1912, no. 15
Anderson 1930(1)
Morris & Bailey 1964, p. 169
Morris 1966, p. 104

Outcrop sheet, 300 m NE of Stellock, 1¼ km NE of Monreith and sea, wide sea views, in grass. First reported by the Royal Commission on Ancient Monuments (1912).

NX 3717 4140 OS: old 80 and Wigtown 31 SW; new 83 and NX 34 SE. 65 m (210 ft).

In the Ward field, 27 m (30 yds) NW of its SE wall, 255 m (280 yds) SE of its NW wall, 270 m (300 yds) NE of the SW wall, 52 m (55 yds) NE of GAL 20 A, is a fairly prominent excrescence. Near its top is uncovered a smooth greywacke outcrop, in 1975 measuring about 3 m by 1¾ m (10 ft × 6 ft), about ⅛ m (½ ft) above field level – horizontal where carved. On it are –

A clear cup-and-five-rings, partly broken off, 45 cm (18 in) diameter and a cup-and-two-rings. There was also visible in 1965 but perhaps weathered off by 1975 a faint cup-and-three-rings. All rings were complete. Greatest carving depth 2 cm (1 in).

There are a stone circle and some standing stones on the farm. The latter are said to have an astronomical significance, when lined up with an island in the bay on mid-winter sunset. They have not been examined by the author.

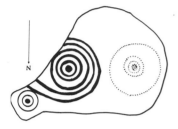

Scale 3:100.

BLAIRBUY 1 — looking E. The smaller carving is just beyond the measuring rod.

BLAIRBUY 2

GAL 16

Outcrop sheet 400 m E of Stellock, 1¼ km NE of Monreith and sea; wide sea views, in grass. First reported by Rev. R. S. G. Anderson 1930).

Anderson 1930(1)
Morris & Bailey 1964,
*   p. 169*
Morris 1966, p. 104

NX 373 412 OS: same sheets and altitude as GAL 15.

In the second field SE of GAL 15 and 255 m (280 yds) SE of it, 65 m (70 yds) SE of the wall, on a long rocky hillock, near its top, is a horizontal greywacke area, uncovered in 1973 for about 2½ m by 1¾. m at ground level (8 ft × 6 ft). On it are –

4 weathered and rather irregularly-shaped cups-and-complete-rings up to four rings, 25 cm (10 in) diameters. In the photograph in the Stranraer Museum a fifth figure is shown – a cup-an -two-complete rings. This may now have weathered off.

BLAIRBUY 2 — looking S. The carvings which were still visible in 1973.

BLAIRBUY 2 — The figure shown in dotted lines at the bottom was not seen in 1964-78, but is in earlier records. Scale 3:100.

BLAIRBUY 2 — two fields E. of Blairbuy 1. Looking N.

Outcrop about 200 m SW of Fell farm's ruins, 2 km NE of Monreith and sea, open sea views, on moor. First discovered by R. McMaster (1967).

Morris 1967, p. 78
Morris 1966, p. 104
Morris 1969, p. 66

NX 374 423 OS: same sheets as GAL 15. 110 m (350 ft).

On Fell of Barhullion's N slope, 16 m (18 yds) S of the corner where 2 walls meet, is one of many greywacke outcrop slabs, 1 m by $\frac{2}{3}$ m, and 1 m high on its W but at turf level elsewhere (3 ft × 2 ft × 3$\frac{1}{2}$ ft). On its smooth top, sloping 25°N are –

A cup-and-six-complete-rings 14 in (35 cm) diameter, the outer one running off the rock's edge, also 3 parallel grooves, the inner one tangential to the outer ring. Greatest carving depth – 1 cm ($\frac{1}{2}$ in).

BLAIRBUY 3 — The 3 tangental parallel lines are an unusual feature of this much-weathered carving.

BLAIRBUY 3 — with its finder, looking N.

BLAIRBUY 4

GAL 18

Outcrop shelf 500 m E of Blairbuy farm ('Blairbuie' on the O.S. maps), 1½ km NE of Monreith and sea, wide sea views, on moor. First discovered by R. McMaster (1968).

Morris 1967, p. 78
Morris 1969, p. 66

NX 368 419 OS: old 80 and Wigtown 30 SE; new 83 and NX 34 SE. 70 m (225 ft).

36 m (40 yds) SW of a wall and 65 m (70 yds) NE of another wall, hard to find in rough rocky ground, is one of many greywacke shelves, smooth and horizontal, bared here for about 3 m by 2 m (10 ft × 6 ft), dropping about 2 m (6 ft) a little to its W, in 2 parts separated by turf – horizontal where carved. On it are –

2 much-weathered cups-and-one-complete-ring 10 cm (4 in) in diameter, and 2 cups, 1 having a possibly natural rectangle round it. Greatest carving depth ¼ cm (⅛ in)

BLAIRBUY 4 — looking S.E. to show the "rectangle". The two much-weathered cups-and-rings can just be seen — at "Y" and "Z".

GAL 19   BLAIRBUY 5

Outcrop sheet 1350 m E of farm, 1½ km NE of Monreith and sea; wide sea views, on moor. First discovered by R. McMaster (1968).

Morris 1967, p. 78
Morris 1969, p. 66

NX 375 417 OS: same sheets as GAL 15. 120 m (420 ft).

180 m (200 yds) ESE of Fell of Barhullion's summit cairn, 135 m (150 yds) E of a gate in the wall, hard to find in rough rocky ground, is a greywacke outcrop shelf ¾ m (2½ ft) high on its NE, at turf level elsewhere, 2¾ m by 1 m (9 ft × 3 ft) sloping 30°E. On it is –

A very clear cup-and-one-complete-ring 10 cm (4 in) diameter, 1 cm (½ in) deep.

BLAIRBUY 5 — the site, looking W.

BLAIRBUY 5 — The very clear cup-and-ring here.

Outcrop 700 m NE of farm, 1½ km NNE of Monreith and sea. Sea views, in rough grass. First discovered by R. McMaster (1976).

NX 367 424 0S: same sheets as GAL 18. 50 m (170 ft).

137 m (150 yds) NW of a farm road, 27 m (30 yds) W of the edge of a small wood, 110 m (124 yds) SW of a field wall, is a greywacke outcrop 2 m by 1½ m, up to ½ m high (6 ft × 5 ft × 1½ ft), sloping 5°N. On it are –

2 cups-and-complete-rings up to 17 cm (7 in) diameter and ½ cm (¼ in) deep, 1 with 1 ring, and 1 with 2 rings and a radial groove from its cup.

BLAIRBUY 6 — the site, looking S.

BLAIRBUY 6 — looking S.E. The spectacles give scale.

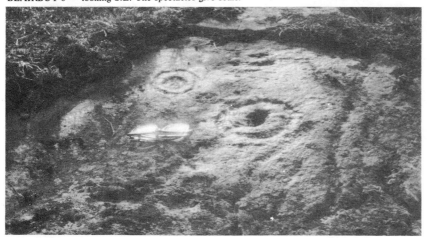

BLAIRBUY 7

Outcrop 270 m E of Stellock, 1½ km NE of Monreith, and sea. Wide sea views. In grass. First noted by the author (1977).

NX 3714 4137 OS: same sheets and altitude as GAL 15.

In the Ward field, 51 m (55 yds) SW of GAL 15, in 1977 the author found that cattle had uncovered a greywacke triangle, horizontal, at ground level, 1 m by 1 m (3 ft × 3 ft). On it are –

A much-weathered cup-and-five-rings and cup-and-three-rings, all incomplete, up to 25 cm (10 in) diameters and ¼ cm (⅛ in) deep. There are faint traces of other cups-and-rings on adjoining newly bared areas, and further excavation may reveal more carvings here.

BLAIRBUY 7 — looking E.

BOMBIE 1 GAL 21

Small outcrop 1150 m ESE of farm, 4 km E of Kirkcudbright and sea; open inland views, in rough grass. First reported by D. C. Bailey (1964).

Morris & Bailey 1964, pp. 165
Morris 1966, p. 104

NX 723 499 OS: old 81 and Kirkcudbright 55 NE; new 83 and NX 74 NW 100 m (325 ft).

In the field 'Rough Tongue of Bombie', 145 m (160 yds)·N of the Dundrennan road, 160 m (175 yds) E of the Gribdae road, on a rocky ridge, is a greywacke outcrop ⅓ m (1 ft) square, at ground level, sloping 20°N, just W of an old quarry. On it is –

A cup-and-seven-complete-rings 34 cm (13 in) diameter, bisected by a groove through the cup. 18 m (20 yds) to its N are 4 'cups' in a line.

Right: BOMBIE 1 — The carving is beside the white can. Looking N.N.E.

Below: BOMBIE 1 — Looking S.E. taken at 9 a.m. The rings are much weathered and show up only in low sun when wet.

GAL 22   BOMBIE 2

Hamilton 1886, p. 159
Coles 1894, p. 82
K. Inventory 1914, no.
  239
Morris & Bailey 1964,
  p. 165
Morris 1966, p. 104

Outcrop in same field as last, similar situation, but now un-traceable. First reported by G. Hamilton (1886).

NX 723 500 OS: same sheets and altitude as last.

In the same field, 'a few yards' S of the Gribdae road, on the ridge nearest the Dundrennan road, in 1886 and 1895 were 4 separate outcrops. On these were –

(a) 6 cups-and-rings, mostly un-gapped, with up to 5 rings, one having a cup in its outer ring.

(b) 3 sets of three concentric rings, 2 with and 1 without a central cup.

(c) 2 cups-and-complete-rings (five and four rings respectively) and a possible one-convolution spiral.

(d) $5\frac{1}{2}$ m (18 ft) NE of this last group – a cup-and-four-rings 30 cm (12 in) diameter.

No scale or measurement is given for any carving except the last.

GAL 23   BROUGHTON MAINS 1

Mann 1915, p. 16
K. Inventory 1912, no.
  507
Morris & Bailey 1964,
  p. 169
Morris 1966, p. 83 and
  104

Outcrop 850 m NE of farm, $5\frac{1}{2}$ km N of Whithorn and $2\frac{1}{2}$ km inland, wide inland views, in grass. First reported by L. M. Mann (1915).

NX 4581 4565 OS: old 80 and Wigtown 31 NE; new 83 and NX 44 NE. 18 m (60 ft).

In the third field E of the farm, 225 m (250 yds) SE of a farm road, 65 m (70 yds) SW of its NE wall, is a rough area of rocks. A grey-wacke outcrop near the S end of this, $5\frac{1}{4}$ m by $5\frac{1}{2}$ m by $\frac{3}{4}$ m high (17 ft × 18 ft × 2 ft), sloping 5°N or horizontal, has, on it –

9 cups-and-rings – up to four rings, some gapped, others not, some 'keyhole-type' with 2 curving radial grooves from the inner ring, 1 ring with no central cup, and at least 11 cups.

BROUGHTON MAINS 1 — looking E.

BROUGHTON MAINS 1 — the Northmost group of carvings, looking E.

BROUGHTON MAINS 1 —
(only approximately correct).

GAL 24   BROUGHTON MAINS 2

Outcrop 300 m WNW of farm, 4½ km N of Whithorn, 2½ km inland, in rough grass, sea views. First noted by I. F. Macleod (1974).

NX 452 453 OS: same sheets and altitude as GAL 23.

100 m (110 yds) NE of the main road's thorn hedge, 170 m (190 yds) NW of the field's wall. When deep-ploughing this field, the farmer found 2 large horizontal greywacke outcrops covered with carvings. Before dynamiting it he reported it to Mr. Macleod, and on his advice has left the rocks untouched. On them are some of Galloway's best-preserved cup-and-ring carvings, and this is a site which ought to be taken into D.O.E. care and re-covered with soil or preservative. The 2 outcrops are about 7 m (7½ yds) apart.

(a) On the larger, NE area, 4½ m by 3 m (15 ft × 10 ft) are – 22 cups-and-rings, having up to 6 concentric rings, some gapped, others not, some with 1–3 radial grooves, mostly from the cup, others with none, also over 30 cups, and some (mostly connecting) grooves. There is also a very small incised 'ladder'.

(b) On the SW area, 3 m by 2 m (10 ft × 6 ft) are – 9 cups-and-rings, having up to 5 rings, some gapped, others not, some with, some without, 1 radial groove from the cup. There are also 2 part-rings, 1 with centre cup, and at least 13 cups and some connecting grooves.

The greatest diameter of a ring is 31 cm (12 in) and carving depths are up to 1 cm (½ in).

The accompanying diagram only shows those parts of the rocks which are carved.

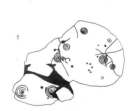

BROUGHTON MAINS 2 — the N.E. area, scale 1:75.

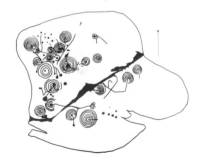

BROUGHTON MAINS 2 — the S.W. area, scale 1:75.

BROUGHTON MAINS 2 — Some of the recently-uncovered carvings. Looking S.

BROUGHTON MAINS 2 — a "close-up" of the strange "ladder". As in all the pictures, the divisions on the scale are 5 cms.

GAL 25   CAIRNHARROW

Coles 1902, p. 219
K. Inventory 1914, no.
  25
Morris & Bailey 1964,
  p. 162
Morris 1966, p. 104
Mann 1915, p. 18

Outcrop 700 m SSW of Cauldside, $4\frac{1}{4}$ km WNW of Anwoth, $4\frac{1}{4}$ km inland, on moor, wide inland views. First reported by F. R. Coles (1902).

NX 541 567 OS: old 80 and Kirkcudbright 47 NE; new 83 and NX 55 NW. 940 ft (285 m).

On the open moor sometimes called Cauldside, hard to find, 300 m (325 yds) SSW of the ruined top end of the wall leading W from Cauldside, just E of a line through Arkland and Glen farms, is a smooth horizontal schist outcrop $2\frac{1}{2}$ m by 1 m, $\frac{3}{4}$ m high on its E, at ground level on its W (8 ft × 3 ft × $2\frac{1}{2}$ ft). On it are –

A cup-and-four-complete-rings with 2 radial grooves from its cup, 40 cm by 38 cm (16 in × 15 in) and 4 smaller cups-and-rings 2 of them gapped, 2 un-gapped, no radial grooves. There are also 9 cups. Greatest carving depth – 1 cm ($\frac{1}{2}$ in).

Parts of this are much weathered, especially the big figure's innermost ring.

CAIRNHARROW — looking S. Arkland farm is in the distance.

CAIRNHARROW — the stone, looking S.

CAIRNHARROW — the carvings chalked in, except for a second radial groove on the large figure, which runs to about "2 o'clock". The top of the picture is S.W.

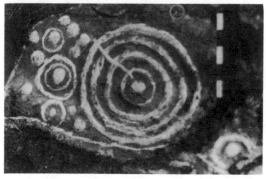

CAIRNHOLY 1-2

Slabs at chambered tomb, 250 m S of farm, 6½ km WSW of Anwoth, ¾ km inland, sea views, in grass (former moor) 1 slab now in the National Museum of Antiquities of Scotland, 1 Queen Street, Edinburgh no. EO 830. First reported by Stuart Piggott and T. G. E. Powell (1948).

NX 5177 5389 OS: old 80 and Kirkcudbright 47 SW; new 83 and NX 55 SW. 135 m (450 ft).

Piggott & Powell 1948, p. 118 & plates 25 & 26
Morris & Bailey 1964, p. 162
Morris 1966, p. 104
K. Inventory 1914, no. 296
Truckell 1961, p. 192

1 Cairnholy 1 is a prominent neolithic tomb, having 2 chambers. Propped up by stones in the SE corner of the inner chamber, and judged to be a secondary insertion, with a food vessel found beside it, was a flat greywacke slab, now in the National Museum, 50 cm by 38 cm by 14 cm (20 in × 15 in × 5½ in). On it is –

A well-preserved cup-and-six-complete-rings, 26 cm (10½ in) diameter and a cup-mark. Greatest carving depth 1 cm (½ in). 3 faint radial grooves run from the cup to the edge – 2 close together.

2 2 m (2 yds) South of this chamber, now lying at an angle with its carved side uppermost, is a flat greywacke slab 1¾ m by 1¼ m by 30 cm (6 ft × 4 ft × 1 ft) which might once have been a cover-slab or other part of the tomb. On it, and so much weathered as only to be visible shortly after mid-day in slanting sun, is –

A partly flaked-off cup-and-five-rings, probably un-gapped, its probable diameter was 31 cm (12½ in), up to ½ cm (¼ in) deep.

CAIRNHOLY 1 — a chambered tomb near Anwoth. The cup-and-ring carved slab in the tomb, now in the National Museum, was in the second chamber behind the two highest uprights. The other carved slab lies on the ground behind, and a little to the left of the uprights.

CAIRNHOLY 1 — the second chamber, in which the first slab was propped up, with a food vessel which can be dated to around 1800 B.C.

CAIRNHOLY 1 — the slab found in the burial chamber.

CAIRNHOLY 2 — the slab — perhaps a cist cover-stone — found beside the tomb. Its carvings, much weathered are just visible in the picture, about its centre.

74

CAIRNHOLY 3

GAL 27

Cube-shaped block found 'about 360 m NE of farm', 6¾ km WSW of Anwoth, 1½ km inland, in rough grass, sea views; now missing. First reported by the Royal Commission on the Ancient Monuments of Scotland (1914).

NX 520 543 OS: old 80 and Kirkcudbright 47 SW; new 83 and NX 55 SW. 130 m (430 ft).

A 'whinstone' (probably greywacke) block, roughly cube-shaped, sides on average about 1½ m (4¾ ft) was ploughed up about 1911 'in the field'. On one face was –
  A cup-and-six-rings 35 cm. (14 in) diameter, 'transversed' by a radial groove. No other details are known.

K. Inventory 1914, no. 296
Morris & Bailey 1964, p. 162
Morris 1966, p. 104
Truckell 1961, p. 192
Piggott & Powell 1948, p. 118

CAIRNHOLY 4

GAL 28

Outcrop shelf 350 m ENE of Kirkmuir farmhouse, 7 km WSW of Anwoth, 1¾ km inland, sea views, in rough grass. First reported by the Royal Commission on Ancient Monuments of Scotland (1914).

NX 5157 5458 OS: same sheets as GAL 26 165 m (550 ft).

155 m (170 yds) N of a field wall, just E of its W wall (the farm boundary) are some greywacke rock outcrops – a low escarpment facing W. 4 areas of this bear carvings –
  (a) A steeply-W-sloping hog-back nearest the W wall bears at least 8 cup-marks, in two parallel rows running roughly NW–SE.
  (b) 2 m (yds) S of this is the northmost cup-and-ring-carved area, 1¾ m by 1¼ m, 2 m high on its N, at ground level on its E, sloping 10°NE where carved. On its fairly smooth surface are –
Parts of a cup-and-three-rings, probably un-gapped, 26 cm (10½ in) diameter, and at least 2 possibly ringed cups.
  (c) 1 m (yd) SE of it is a horizontal area 1 m by ½ m, up to 13 cm high (3¼ ft × 1½ ft × 5 in). On it are –
A cup-and-two-complete-rings 17 cm (6½ in) diameter, and 11 cups.
  (d) 1 m (yd) SE of this is another horizontal area, 3 m by 2 m by 1½ m high on its W, less elsewhere. On it are –
A cup-and-three-rings, 3 cups-and-two-rings, and at least 10 cups. Probably all the rings are un-gapped. Greatest diameter – 25 cm (10 in).

K. Inventory 1914, no. 296
Morris & Bailey 1964, p. 162
Morris 1966, p. 104

There is a cast of a cup-and-three-rings in the National Museum of Antiquities, Edinburgh, no IA 38, which is probably from this site but now under turf. It shows a cup as 'runner' in its inner ring, with a groove leading thence to the centre.

Many of the carvings are much weathered – greatest carving depth is now 3 cm (1¼ in).

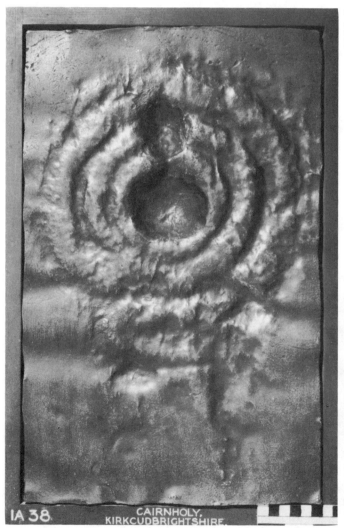

CAIRNHOLY 4 — a cast now in the National Museum of Antiquities of Scotland, Edinburgh, almost certainly of a carving here, now turf-covered or broken off. Photograph by courtesy of the Museum.

CAIRNHOLY 4 — rock "(B)", looking S.W.

CAIRNHOLY 5

Slab 550 m NE of Kirkmuir farmhouse, in same field and situation as last. First reported by the Royal Commission on Ancient Monuments of Scotland (1912).

K. Inventory 1914, no. 296
Morris & Bailey 1964, p. 162
Morris 1966, p. 104

NX 516 547 OS: same sheets and altitude as last.

230 m (250 yds) NNE of the stones GAL 28, 145 m (160 yds) W of the field's wall, 110 m (120 yds) S of another of its walls, is a stony area. In it is a smooth flat-topped and horizontal greywacke slab $1\frac{1}{2}$ m by $\frac{1}{2}$ m by 30 cm thick ($5\frac{1}{4}$ ft × 2 ft × 1 ft). On its upper surface, as now lying, are –

At least 3 much-weathered cups-and-four-complete-rings, greatest diameter 35 cm ($13\frac{1}{2}$ in) and depths up to $1\frac{1}{2}$ cm ($\frac{3}{4}$ in) and 2 cups.

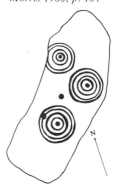

Scale 3:100.

CAIRNHOLY 5 — looking N.W. The carvings here are very much weathered.

GAL 30

CAIRNHOLY 6

Morris & Bailey 1964,
p. 162
Morris 1966, p. 104

850 m NE of Kirkmuir farmhouse, 6¼ km W of Anwoth, 2 km inland, sea views, on moor, now missing. First reported by the author (1964).

NX 517 550 OS: old 80 and Kirkcudbright 47 NW; new 83 and NX 55 NW. 180 m (600 ft).

180 m (200 yds) E of a stone sheepfold, 9 m (10 yds) N of a wall, about 10 cm (4 in) below ground level, in a field drain which had been newly dug in 1964, the author noted a pointed greywacke rock ½ m by ¼ m (2 ft × 1 ft), sloping where carved 10°E. On it was –

A much-weathered cup-and-one-complete-ring 18 cm (7 in) diameter, of negligible depth.

This must since then have become re-covered and cannot now be found for photography, however a rubbing was made.

CAIRNHOLY 6 — a rubbing of this stone, found when draining the moor, and now covered again by heather and turf.

CAMBRET MOOR

Slab 1500 m NE of Cambret, 5¼ km WNW of Anwoth, 4¾ km inland, sea views, in rough grass. First reported by W. Mackenzie (1841).

Mackenzie 1841, p. 47
Simpson 1864
Simpson 1867, p. 36
 ('Camerot')
K. Inventory 1914, no.
 295
McWhite 1946, p. 79
Morris & Bailey 1964,
 p. 162
Morris 1966, p. 104
Hadingham 1974, p. 74
Coles 1898, p. 368

NX 528 574 OS: old 80 and Kirkcudbright 47 NE; new 83 and NX 55 NW. 230 m (750 ft).

295 m (320 yds) NNW of the neolithic Cauldside cairn, on the moor's E slope, is a greywacke slab 1¼ m by 1 m by ⅓ m high (4¼ ft × 3 ft × 14 in) sloping 20°SE. On its smooth top are –

A cup-and-one-complete-ring, surrounded by a six-convolution spiral, with a radial groove from its cup, which seems to break some of the convolutions' continuity, 58 cm (23 in) diameter, and also a very faint, weathered, incomplete, cup-and-three-rings. Greatest carving depth ½ cm (¼ in).

A slab 27 m (30 yds) NW has been split along a line of small 'cup-marks', and cup-marked stones have been found in the neolithic cairn and near it. A stone circle is also near.

Below: CAMBRET MOOR — the carved slab, looking E. *Left:* CAMBRET MOOR — the much-weathered cup-and-ring on the right is barely visible. But the big spiral is clearly seen when wet, although also much weathered. Looking S.E. *Left below:* CAMBRET MOOR — the carvings chalked in, looking N.

GAL 33   CASTLECREAVIE

Coles 1894, p. 83
Morris & Bailey 1964,
  p. 165
Morris 1966, p. 104

Outcrop on Castlecreavie, 4 km ESE of Kirkcudbright and sea, in rough grass, now missing. First reported by F. R. Coles (1894).

NX 72 49 OS: old 81 and Kirkcudbright 55 NE; new 83 and NX 74 NW. 120 m (400 ft).

S of the public road, and a few score yards W of the loaning (presumably at the now deserted farmhouse), within a foot ($\frac{1}{3}$ m) of broken rock at the E edge of a quarry, Coles in 1894 found carved –
    A cup-and-four-rings, a cup, and two probable 'dumb-bells'. These have not been seen since before 1911, and may either have flaked off or been quarried. There is a quarry 570 m (625 yds) NNE of the farm.

GAL 34   CLAUCHANDOLLY 1

Coles 1894, p. 87
K. Inventory 1914, no.
  66
Morris & Bailey 1964,
  p. 164
Breuil 1934, p. 316
Morris 1966, p. 106
Mann 1915, p. 17

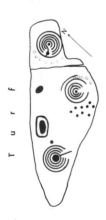

Outcrop shelf 400 m SW of Clauchendolly smithy ruins, in Brighouse farm's 'Cleich' field, 1½ km SE of Borgue, 1¼ km inland, sea views, in good grass. First reported by F. R. Coles (1894).

NX 6424 4714 OS: old 80 and Kirkcudbright 54 SE; new 83 and NX 64 NW. 20 m (70 ft).

In a hollow, 45 m (50 yds) SE of a wall, 85 m (95 yds) N of another wall, is a fairly smooth greywacke shelf, curving NE, 15° where carved, 1½ m by ¾ m 30 cm high on its NE, nil elsewhere (5 ft × 2½ ft × 1 ft). On it are –
    3 much-weathered gapped cups-and-rings, 2 with 4 and 1 with 5 rings. The cup in the SW figure is a hollowed-out flat disc. The ring gaps in the middle figure leave a bare flat space. The 2 side figures have radial grooves from the inner ring, but the NE one's outer ring is un-gapped and the groove ends there. There is also an unusual ringed oval and another oval. In 1894 there were 24 cups, some of them partly ringing the 2 NE figures; but in 1974 only those SW of the centre figure could be seen in low sun. Greatest ring diameter 25 cm (10 in) and carving depth ¼ cm (⅛ in).

CLAUCHANDOLLY 1 — the un-blacked circles represent former cup-marks not traced in 1974. Scale 3:100.

CLAUCHANDOLLY 1 — looking S.W. on a winter evening.

CLAUCHANDOLLY 1 — looking S. The field is less flat than it seems.

CLAUCHANDOLLY 2   GAL 35

Small outcrop 250 m SW of the ruined smithy, in same situation as last. First reported by the Royal Commission on Ancient Monuments of Scotland (1911).

NX 644 472 OS: same sheets and altitude as last.

Hard to find, in the same field 135 m (150 yds) from its NE corner, 86 m (96 yds) from its E wall, is a small rough ridge-like greywacke outcrop 60 cm by 30 cm at ground level (2 ft × 1 ft). On it is –
    A cup-and-two-rings (incomplete) 20 cm (8 in) diameter and up to 1 cm ($\frac{1}{2}$ in) deep.

K. Inventory 1914, no. 66
Morris & Bailey 1964, p. 164
Morris 1966, p. 106

CLAUCHANDOLLY 2 — looking towards the Smithy (now in ruins).

CLAUCHANDOLLY 2 — looking S.

CLAUCHANDOLLY 3

GAL 36

Outcrop about 450 m SSW of the ruined smithy, in same situation as GAL 34. First reported by the Royal Commission on Ancient Monuments of Scotland (1911), now missing.

K. Inventory 1914, no. 66
Morris & Bailey 1964, p. 164
Morris 1966, p. 106

NX 64 47 OS: same sheets and altitude as GAL 34.

In the same field as **GAL 35**, 9 m (30 ft) S of the highest point of – and near the E end of – a long prominent ridge on the S side of the hollow where GAL 34 lies, was found, carved on outcrop (probably greywacke) –

A hollowed disc 5 cm (2 in) diameter surrounded by 5 rings up to 25 cm (10 in) diameter, and a cup-and-one-ring.

This cannot now be traced, and may have been re-covered with earth. No further details are known.

CLAUCHANDOLLY 6

GAL 38

Outcrop about 300 m SW of the smithy, in the same situation as GAL 34. First reported by I. F. McLeod (1969).

McLeod 1969, p. 29

NX 6438 4711 OS: same sheets and altitude as GAL 34.

In the same field, on a rocky un-cultivated hillock, 4 m (4½ yds) SE of an electric pylon and about 235 m (250 yds) W of the main road, is a horizontal greywacke outcrop, 1½ m by ⅓ m just below ground level (5 ft × 1 ft) – hard to find. On it are –

A cup-and-two-complete-rings 10 cm (4 in) diameter, with traces of a third ring showing on making a rubbing, a cup with traces of a possible ring, and at least 4 other cups – up to ½ cm (¼ in) deep.

12¼ m (14 yds) S of this outcrop is another cup-marked outcrop.

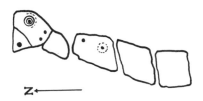

CLAUCHANDOLLY 6 — Only faint traces are visible of the dotted features. Scale 3:100.

CLAUCHANDOLLY 6 — looking S.

GAL 39   CLAUCHANDOLLY 8

McLeod 1969, p. 29

Outcrop 150 m SW of the smithy, in same situation as GAL 34. First reported by I. F. McLeod (1969).

NX 6447 4722 OS: same sheets and altitude as GAL 34.

5 m (5½ yds) W of the same field's E wall, 73 m (80 yds) S of its N wall, on a small rock ridge running NE, is a greywacke outcrop 1¼ m by ¾ m, ⅓ m high on its W, ground level elsewhere (4 ft × 2½ ft × 1 ft) – horizontal where carved. On it are –

A cup with possible ring round it, a cup-and-four-complete-rings and a cup-and-one-complete-ring, all in line, and an incomplete, much-weathered, cup-and-five-rings. Greatest diameter 20 cm (8 in) and depth ¼ cm (⅛ in).

Above: CLAUCHANDOLLY 8 — looking N.E., towards the ruined Smithy.
Below: CLAUCHANDOLLY 8 — looking S.

Right: CLAUCHANDOLLY 8 — Only faint traces are visible of the dotted features. Scale 3:100.

GAL 40   CLAUCHANDOLLY 9

Outcrop ridge 400 m SSW of the smithy, in the same situation as GAL 34. First noted by the author (1972).

NX 644 469 OS: same sheets as GAL 34. 80 m (160 ft).

In the NE corner of the second field S of the smithy, being the second field W of the main road, 2 m (2 yds) W of its wall and 42 m (46 yds) S of the other wall, is a rather cylindrical greywacke outcrop, here exposed for 4½ m by 1½ m (15 ft × 5 ft) at ground level, curving with the ground up to about 30°W. On its horizontal smooth top, near the NE end, are –

Parts of a much-weathered cup-and-two-rings 23 cm (9 in) diameter, the cup being 2 cm (1 in) deep.

CLAUCHANDOLLY 9 — Looking N.

CLAUCHANDOLLY 9 — the carvings chalked in.

CLAUNCH 1

GAL 41

Outcrop 'table' 120 m SE of farm, 1¾ km NNW of Sorbie, 3¼ km inland, open views, in pasture. First reported by the Royal Commission on Ancient Monuments of Scotland (1911).

W. Inventory 1914, no. 424
Morris & Bailey 1964, p. 169
Morris 1966, p. 106

NX 427 481 OS: old 80 and Wigtown 36 SE; new 83 and NX 44 NW. 35 m (120 ft).

21 m (23 yds) N of a field wall is a greywacke raised, horizontal, table or mound 3 m by 2½ m by ⅓ m high at most (10 ft × 8 ft × 1 ft), smooth but with big turf-filled cracks. On it are –

2 cups-and-two-rings, 6 cups-and-one-ring, at least 7 cups and some grooves. Some rings are gapped, others not, some of each kind have a radial groove from cup or inner ring, others not. Greatest ring diameter 20 cm (8 in) and carving depths up to 2 cm (1 in).

CLAUNCH 1 — looking N.W. towards the farm. The carvings are much weathered, except the one in the foreground.

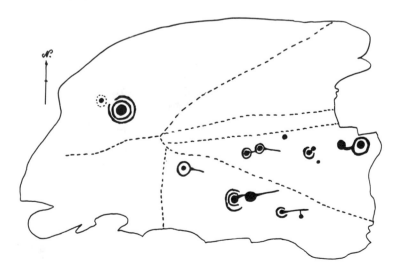

CLAUNCH 1 — Scale 3:100.

GAL 42   CLAUNCH 2

Morris & Bailey 1964
p. 169
Morris 1966, p. 106

Outcrop shelf 360 m NNE of the farm, 2 km NNW of Sorbie, 3¼ km inland, open views, in pasture. First reported by the author (1964).

NX 4290 4845 OS: same sheets and altitude as last above.

25 m (27 yds) E of a field's wall (OS no 302), and 60 m (70 yds) NW from its gate a greywacke ridge emerges from the turf in places, and here, at a smooth horizontal part exposed for 1¼ m by ⅓ m, ½ m high on its S, at ground level elsewhere (4 ft × 1 ft × 2 ft), are –

2 well-preserved cups-and-three-complete-rings, the third ring in the larger carving being unfinished, and its diameter (if the ring had been finished) being 33 cm (13 in). Greatest carving depth 1 cm (½ in).

There is a cup-marked boulder over the wall to the NW in the little wood.

CLAUNCH 2 — looking S.S.W., towards the farm.

CLAUNCH 2 — looking S.E.

CRAIGNARGET

Slab 'from Craignarget', 8½ km SE of Glenluce, near the sea, now in the National Museum of Antiquities, Edinburgh, no. IB 43. First reported by Mrs. Young M'Dowall (1880).

Young M'Dowall 1880, p. 250–1.
Wilson 1898, p. 173
Morris 1966, p. 106
Mann 1915, p. 28

NX 25 51 OS: old 79 and Wigtown 24 NE; new 82 and NX 25 SE.

In 1880 Mrs. M'Dowall presented to the Society of Antiquaries of Scotland a greywacke slab found on the farm, 1 m by ½ m (3½ ft × 1½ ft), 8.5 cm (3½ in) thick. On it were:

5 crosses, each with a cup at each end, the biggest being 45 cm by 30 cm (18 in × 12 in) with a cup-and-one-complete-ring in its centre, also 4 circles (some incomplete), 9 incomplete ringed ovals (some with double rings), a swastika with cups at each angle and end, and 21 cups.

This is almost certainly an Early Christian carving, and its site is somewhat further West than any of the older series of cups-and-rings in Galloway.

Another 'sculptured slab' was found at the same site, but it was broken up and used for building a byre. No other details are known.

CULDOACH

Outcrop slabs 1450 m S of the farm, 2¼ km E of Kirkcudbright, and sea, wide views, in rough grass. First reported by F. R. Coles (1894).

Coles 1894, p. 85
K. Inventory 1914, no. 249
(Little Stockerton)
Morris & Bailey 1964, p. 166
Morris 1966, p. 106

NX 7083 5250 OS: old 81 and Kirkcudbright 49 SW; new 83 and NX 75 SW. 100 m (325 ft).

63 m (70 yds) from a field's N wall, 182 m (200 yds) from its W wall and 310 m (340 yds) NW of road B727, is a big rocky knoll. Its SE side has some smooth greywacke slabs sloping 35°SE. On an area of these about 11 m by 4 m, at ground level but 1½ m high on its W (35 ft × 12 ft × 5 ft), interspersed with turf, are –

At least 19 cups-and-rings, some much weathered, having one to four rings, some gapped, others not, some with a radial groove from the cup, others not, and at least 21 cups. Some of these may have been ringed. On the W slab there is a pleasing effort at design. Greatest ring diameter 25 cm (9½ in) and carving depths up to ½ cm (¼ in).

45 m (50 yds) further SE there is a rock bearing a line of 8 cups, which may have been made in an attempt to split it.

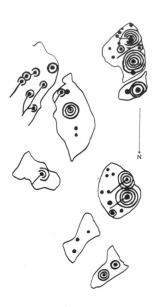

CULDOACH — looking N. The smooth slabs are covered with carvings.

CULDOACH — Scale 3:100.

CULDOACH — some of the carvings, looking S — the S.W. area.

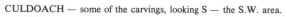

CULNOAG

Outcrop slab 75 m E of Doonhill farmhouse, $1\frac{3}{4}$ km E of Sorbie, 4 km inland; sea views, in rough grass. First reported by the author (1976).

NX 417 469 OS: old 80 and Wigtown 26 SW; new 83 and NX 44 NW. 55 m (180 ft)

30 m (35 yds) E of the road's wall, 27 m (30 yds) NNW of another wall, in a rough area, is a smooth greywacke outcrop, $1\frac{1}{2}$ m by 1 m, just below ground level ($4\frac{1}{2}$ ft × 3 ft), sloping 10° ESE. On it are –

9 much-weathered and now incomplete cups-and-rings, having up to 6 rings, and at least 12 cups. Greatest ring diameter 27 cm ($10\frac{1}{2}$ in) and carving depths up to 1 cm ($\frac{1}{2}$ in).

CULNOAG — Scale 3:100.

CULNOAG — the stone, chalked in, looking W, towards Doonhill farm.

CULNOAG — the stone, looking W, just before sunset — the carvings like so many in Galloway, are much weathered.

DRUMMORAL

Anderson 1926, pp. 119–121
Morris & Bailey 1964, p. 170
Morris 1966, p. 106

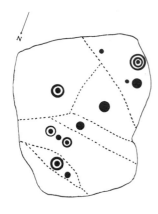

Outcrop table 600 m NNE of the farm, 4 km SSE of Whithorn, 1¼ km inland, open views, in rough grass. First reported by the Rev. R. S. G. Anderson (1926).

NX 464 367 OS: old 80 and Wigtown 35 SE; new 83 and NX 43 NE. 60 m (200 ft).

In the Forrans field, 90 m (100 yds) from its N wall, 90 m (100 yds) from its E wall, is one of many gorse-covered hillocks, on top of which is a greywacke table-like sheet, now at turf level, 1⅓ m by 1¼ m (4½ ft × 4¼ ft), sloping 10°N. On its smooth but fissured top are –

A cup-and-two-complete-rings, 15 cm (6 in) diameter, 4 cups-and-one-complete-ring and at least 7 cups. Greatest carving depth – 1 cm (½ in). All except the first of these are much weathered.

DRUMMORAL — the dotted lines show the main cracks. Scale 3:100.

DRUMMORAL — the rock's Southmost corner, looking S.

DRUMTRODDAN 1   GAL 47

Outcrop 200 m S of the farm, 2¾ km ENE of Port William and sea; open views, in pasture. First reported by F. R. Coles (1902).

NX 362 447 OS: old 80 and Wigtown 30 NE; new 83 and NX 34 SE. 67 m (220 ft).

Coles 1902, p. 222
Coles 1905, p. 327
Mann 1915, p. 14
Feachem 1963, p. 91
W. Inventory 1912, no. 225
Morris & Bailey 1964, p. 170
Morris 1966, pp. 91 & 106
Paturi 1976, p. 157 & Karte 4

Inside the NW of the 2 small fenced enclosures in mid-field, are scattered a number of greywacke outcrops, quite close together. Many of them, shown on the plan, bear much-weathered carvings, all on areas sloping 25° or less. They cover about 11 m by 10 m (12¼ yds × 11 yds) and rise at most to about 1 m (3 ft) above ground level. While there are probably more, the author, during eight visits, has been able to note, as shown on the plan –

84 cups-and-rings, the number of rings varying from 1 to 6. Some rings are complete, others incomplete or gapped. Some have a radial groove from the cup or a ring, others have none. There are also at least 65 cups (some possibly ringed) and some connecting grooves. Most carvings are on surfaces sloping about 10°N. Greatest diameter – 38 cm (15 in) and carving depths up to 2 cm (1 in).

Right: DRUMTRODDAN 1 — the site, looking S.S.W. A great many of the rocks here are carved.

DRUMTRODDAN 1 — the Eastern end, looking S.

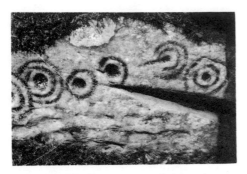

DRUMTRODDAN 1 — some of the carvings, showing the variation of design — gapped and un-gapped rings, some with, others without, a radial groove, all close together.

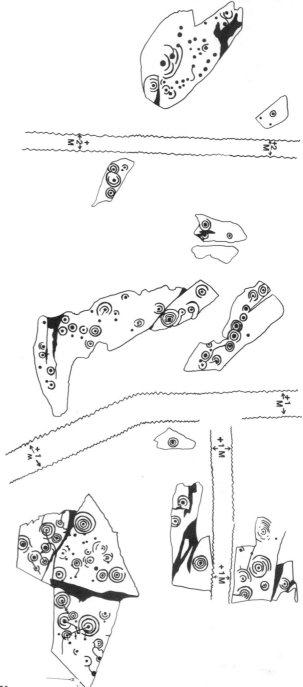

DRUMTRODDAN 1 — scale 1:75.

DRUMTRODDAN 2

GAL 48

Outcrops 20 m (22 yds) SE of last above, in same situation. First noted by the Department of the Environment (1962–1977).

Feachem 1963, p. 91
Morris & Bailey 1964,
  p. 170
Morris 1966, p. 106

NX 362 447 OS: same sheets and altitude as last above.

Inside the SE of the two enclosures are several boulder-like grey-wacke outcrops, the biggest being $1\frac{1}{4}$ m by $\frac{3}{4}$ m by $\frac{1}{4}$ m high (4 ft × $2\frac{1}{2}$ ft × $\frac{3}{4}$ ft). In the first 3 of these noted below the carved face slopes 10–20°N. On them respectively are –

(a) On the biggest outcrop – a cup-and-five-complete-rings, with a radial groove downwards from cup to ground.

(b) 3 m ($3\frac{1}{3}$ yds) to its S – a cup-and-five-rings with 2 faint parallel grooves, both probably from the cup, and also a cup-and-four-complete-rings with a natural bisecting groove.

(c) 4 m ($4\frac{1}{2}$ yds) SW of (a) – a cup-and-six-complete-rings with a natural bisecting groove. This, 35 cm ($13\frac{1}{2}$ in) diameter, is the biggest carving in the group.

(d) $6\frac{1}{2}$ m (7 yds) SW of (a) is a group of 4 very faint cups-and-rings, 2 with 5 rings, 1 with 3 rings, and 1 with 2 rings, all on a face sloping 5°SW, and much weathered.

(b), (c) and (d) are all recent finds by the Scottish Development Department, which has extended its enclosure to include them.

DRUMTRODDAN 2 — the biggest of the carved outcrops, looking S.

GAL 49   DRUMTRODDAN 3

Morris & Bailey 1964,
p. 170 & plate XXII
Morris 1966, p. 106

Outcrops 250 m SSW of the farm in same situation as the last two above. First reported by the author (1964).

NX 361 446 OS: same sheets as last. 70 m (230 ft).

Over the wall, in the wood, about 90 m (100 yds) WSW of the above, 6 m (yds) WSW of the wall, 50 m (55 yds) N of another wall, 2 grey-wacke areas have recently been uncovered –

(a) On an area $3\frac{1}{2}$ m by 3 m (12 ft × 10 ft) at ground level, sloping 15°NW are –

A cup-and-five-complete-rings 71 cm (28 in) diameter, 4 cups-and-three-rings, much weathered, probably complete, 2 with a radial groove from the cup, and at least 14 cups, some of which have traces of having been ringed. Greatest carving depth 1 cm ($\frac{1}{2}$ in).

(b) 3 m (yds) SSE of it is a small outcrop 1 m by $\frac{1}{2}$ m at ground level, sloping 15°SW. On it are –

A cup-and-three-incomplete-rings (broken off) 25 cm (10 in) diameter, and 2 possibly ringed cups. Greatest carving depth 1 cm ($\frac{1}{2}$ in).

Further excavation in this area may well reveal more carvings.

DRUMTRODDAN 3 — Looking S. The bucket marks site "B".

DRUMTRODDAN 3 — The biggest carving, 71 cm diameter.

DRUMTRODDAN 3 — the S.S.E. area, ("B").

Morris & Bailey 1964,
p. 168
Morris 1966, pp. 83 &
106

Outcrop 500 m ENE of the farm, 4½ km NE of Dalry, 30 km inland, wide views, in rough grass. First reported by J. Williams (1964).

NX 662 837 OS: old 73 and Kirkcudbright 18 NE; new 77 and NX 68 SE. 230 m (750 ft).

200 m (220 yds) E of the corner where 2 walls meet, 27 m (30 yds) S of the wall running up Knockmain burn, is a horizontal smooth greywacke outcrop slab, visible from the road below, 2 m by 1¼ m, 15 cm high (7 ft × 4 ft × ½ ft). On it are –

7 very shallow, lightly pecked, circles with no cup. 3 have parts of a second concentric ring and one has parts of a third. Greatest diameter – 33 cm (13 in). There are also some grooves and a perhaps natural basin 27 cm (10½ in) diameter and 15 cm (6 in) deep, and – on a shelf below the SW corner – a smaller basin.

Such rings without central cups are very unusual on outcrop carvings in Galloway.

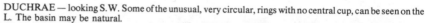

DUCHRAE — looking S.W. Some of the unusual, very circular, rings with no central cup, can be seen on the L. The basin may be natural.

DUCHRAE — looking S.W., with the carvings chalked in.

ELRIG (House of)

Small block built into the house, 6½ km NNW of Port William, 2½ km inland. First reported by the author (1964).

NX 312 495 OS: old 80 and Wigtown 25 SE; new 83 and NX 34 NW. 105 m (350 ft).

'Found nearby' and built into the East Bay of the house's outside wall ½ m (2 ft) below the first floor window, about 1917, is a grey-wacke block 25 cm by 10 cm (10 in × 4 in). On its outer face are –

2 concentric rings (no centre cup), the outer ring gapped with 2 radial grooves ('keyhole type'), the inner complete, with a radial groove parallel with the others. Greatest diameter 10 cm (4 in) and carving depth ½ cm (¼ in).

Morris & Bailey 1964, p. 170
Morris 1966, pp. 83 & 108

GAL 51

a rubbing of the carving.

Small outcrop 350 m SSW of the farm, 2 km N of Whithorn, 3 km inland, wide views, in pasture. First reported by the Rev. G. Wilson (1898).

Coles 1898, p. 371
W. Inventory 1912, no. 508
Morris & Bailey 1964, p. 170

McWhite 1946, p. 80
Morris 1966, p. 83 & 108
Morris 1973, p. 165

NX 448 420 OS: old 80 and Wigtown 31 SE; new 83 and NX 44 SW. 70 m (230 ft).

18 m (20 yds) SE of the farm road's wall, 113 m (125 yds) SW of another wall, sometimes turf-covered and hard to find, is a smooth horizontal greywacke outcrop, partly exposed in 1964–1974 for about $4\frac{1}{2}$ m by $\frac{2}{3}$ m (15 ft × 2 ft), at ground level. Towards its W end is –

A well-preserved S-shaped single spiral, $3\frac{1}{2}$ convolutions at one end and 2 at the other, 30 cm by 18 cm (12 in × 7 in) surrounded by a partly natural parallelogram of grooves.

The cast of this in the National Museum of Antiquities, Edinburgh is no. IA 27.

It is said that other carvings – cups-and-rings – have been found in this field, but no details are known and they are almost certainly turf-covered at present.

GALLOWS OUTON — the "S" spiral.

GALTWAY 1~4 GAL 53~56

Outcrops W of Galtway village ruins, 4 km ESE of Kirkcudbright, 3 km inland, open views, in rough grass. First reported by F. R. Coles (1894).

Coles 1894, pp. 79–81
K. Inventory 1914, no. 251
Morris & Bailey 1964, p. 166
Morris 1966, p. 108

NX 70 48 OS: old 81 and Kirkcudbright 55 SW; new 83 and NX 74 NW. 105–135 m (350–450 ft).

On some of the many greywacke outcrops and rocks on Galtway hill Coles noted 4 groups of carvings; but none of these have been traceable since at least 1911. The data given by Coles are as follows –
GAL 53 (a) A cup-and-three-incomplete-rings 28 cm (11 in) in diameter, with 3 radial grooves, 1 from the cup, 1 from the inner ring, and 1 somewhere between.

(b) About a metre (yd) N of this – a cup-and-three-complete-rings, the outer one being broken at the rock's edge.

(c) 3 m (10 ft) E of (a), a cup-and-four-complete-rings.

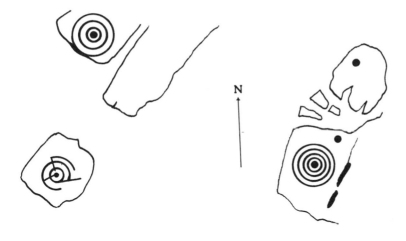

N

GALTWAY 1 — From F. R. Coles' sketch of this group, now untraceable. No scale was given, but the distance between the 2 Western carvings and the Eastern one is given as about 3 m. (10 ft.).

GAL 54 'Several hundred yards (metres) E of these, at Galtway Hill's base' are 16 cups, some connected by grooves, and one having a groove round it forming more than a semi-circle.

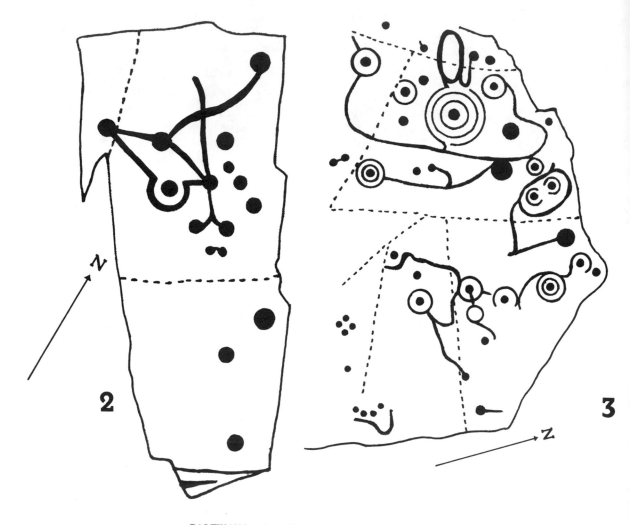

GALTWAY 2 — From Coles' sketch of what he found. Scale unknown. The cracks are shown as hatched lines.

GALTWAY 3 — From Coles sketch of what he found. Scale unknown. The cracks are shown as hatched lines.

GAL 55 'At the base of the same hill', on an outcrop sloping WNW –

12 cups-and-rings, mostly complete rings, but some incomplete, 1 with 3 rings, 2 with 2 rings, the others with 1. In one case 2 sets are enclosed in one second oval ring, and there are also a ring and an oval, both without a central cup, some connecting grooves and 29 cups.

GAL 56 'Higher ... and to the East of ... the last', partly on a saddle-back of rock, are –

6 cups-and-rings, having between 7 and 1 concentric rings. 4 of these have complete rings. 2 are gapped or incomplete. 2 of the former have a radial groove from the cup. There are also 13 cups. Greatest diameter 50 cm (20 in).

Coles gives no other details or measurements for these Galtway carvings, all of which seem now to be un-traceable. But see **GAL 84 and 85** – the descriptions of the 2 sites on Low Banks farm have similarities, although the carvings there are different.

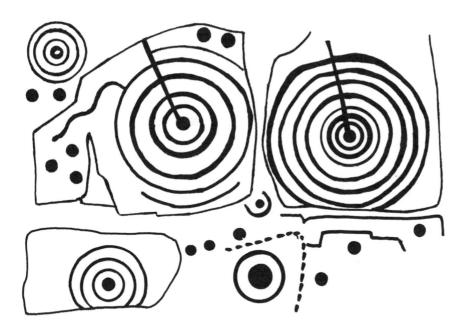

GALTWAY 4 — From F. R. Coles' sketch of what he found, now untraceable. Scale and compass bearing unknown; but, clearly, different scales have been used, as the diameters of the 2 largest figures is given by him as 20 in. and 12½ in. (50 cm and 32 cm).

GAL 57

GILLROANIE

Hamilton 1886, p. 157
Coles 1894, p. 76
K. Inventory 1914, no. 244
Morris & Bailey 1964, p. 166
Morris 1966, p. 108

SE of and near the farm, 3½ km SSE of Kirkcudbright, 2 km inland, sea views. In boulder-strewn area. First reported by G. Hamilton (1886).

NX 701 481 OS: old 81 and Kirkcudbright 55 SW; new 83 and NX 74 NW. 105 m (350 ft)

'Near Gillroanie, in a field to the SE, close to the edge of a quarry' (the quarry is still there), on a rock steeply sloping NE, with a vertical NW face, are said to be –

A horse-shoe shape with cup in centre, and an oval – size unknown.

Although searched for since 1911 by the Royal Commission on Ancient Monuments of Scotland, the Ordnance Survey, the author and others, it has been impossible to trace this rock; yet the farmer states that a local party come to the quarry every three years to examine it.

GILLROANIE — from the sketch by F. R. Coles, scale unknown. This stone, said to have a carved vertical face on its N.W., has not been traced either in 1911, or in 1964-78 by the author. But it is believed that its whereabouts — covered over or uncovered — are known to some local people.

GLASSERTON MAINS

GAL 58

Outcrop 1100 m SW of the Home Farm, 5 km SW of Whithorn, 1 km inland, sea views, in pasture. First reported by the Royal Commission on Ancient Monuments of Scotland (1911).

W. Inventory 1914, no. 17
Morris & Bailey 1964, p. 170
Morris 1966, p. 82 & 108

NX 406 373 OS: old 80 and Wigtown 35 NW; new 83 and NX 43 NW. 95 m (310 ft)

In the field W of the wood, 80 m (88 yds) NE of its SW gate, 215 m (235 yds) from its NW wall, 65 m (70 yds) from its SW wall, is a greywacke outcrop $13\frac{1}{2}$ m by $4\frac{1}{2}$ m, $1\frac{1}{2}$ m high on its SW, at ground level on its NE (45 ft × 15 ft × 5 ft). On its smooth surface, sloping 15°SE, are –

At least 18 cups-and-rings (up to four rings), some gapped, others not, some with, others without, one radial groove from the cup, also 2 cups. A cup-and-three-gapped-rings on a separate block, 1 m by 1 m, which is 1 m to the E seems to have been incised. The SW vertical face has been split off, as has been done with some other rocks around Whithorn, along a row of cup-like holes, close together. Greatest ring diameter 28 cm (11 in) and carving depths up to 1 cm ($\frac{1}{2}$ in). Some carvings are now very faint.

From the site, which is hard to find otherwise, Big Scar Island is in line through the gate.

GLASSERTON MAINS — the carved areas looking S.E.

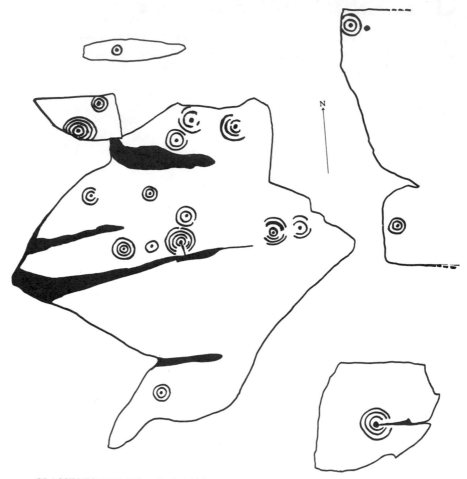

GLASSERTON MAINS — Scale 3:100.

GLASSERTON MAINS — The S.E. figure, which may have been incised perhaps at a later date.

GLENTROOL

Slab 1200 m N of ruined Culsharg, 17 km N of Newton Stewart and sea, on heather moor, open views. First noted by A. Murray an G. Wood (1972).

NX 412 833 OS: old 73 and Kirkcudbright 16; new 77 and NX 48 SW. 550 m (1800 ft).

Using the path from Glentrool to Merrick, marked by white posts, 270 m (300 yds) N of a sheep fence there is a prominent permanent dark green mossy patch. 65 m (70 yds) NNW of it, invisible from the track, is a 3 ft (1 m) high cairn. 1 m (yd) N of it is a horizontal smooth andesite slab $2\frac{1}{4}$ m by $1\frac{1}{2}$ m, $\frac{1}{4}$ m high on its S, at ground level on its N ($7\frac{1}{2}$ ft × $5\frac{1}{2}$ ft × 1 ft). On it are –

A cup-and-one-complete-ring 11 cm ($4\frac{1}{2}$ in) diameter, 2 cm (1 in) deep, probably incised, and little weathered. There are also some incised straight lines up to 50 cm (20 in) long, some at angles to each other. Similar lines have been noticed by the author on other stones in Galloway, but not noted specifically unless accompanied by other carvings.

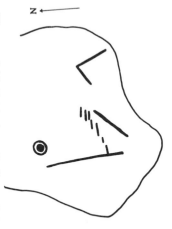

GLENTROOL — Scale 3:100.

GLENTROOL — looking S. Only the line on the R showed up in the only sunshine available for photography — on the author's third visit.

GAL 60

THE GRANGE

Coles 1894, pp. 73–75
K. Inventory 1914, no.
  243
Morris & Bailey 1964,
  p. 166
Morris 1966, p. 108

Outcrops 400 m S of the Grange, 4 km S of Kirkcudbright, $\frac{3}{4}$ km inland, sea views, in pasture. First reported by F. R. Coles (1894).

NX 687 471 OS: old 80 and Kirkcudbright 55 SW; new 83 and NX 64 NE. 30 m (100 ft).

260 m (280 yds) WSW of the road, 9 m (10 yds) NE of the SW hedge of the second field S of the Grange, on a rocky escarpment $3\frac{1}{2}$ m (12 ft) high on its SW, over an area of about 9 m by 3 m (30 ft × 10 ft), at ground level, there are the following greywacke carved outcrop sheets – all close together –

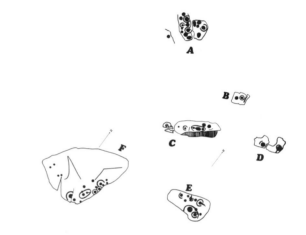

GRANGE — Scale 1:75.

Rock A – horizontal – has 4 cups-and-one-gapped-ring and at least 1 has a radial groove from its cup, also 12 cups.

Rock B – horizontal – has a cup-and-one-complete-ring and a cup.

Rock C – sloping 5°SW – has 2 cups-and-one gapped-ring, 3 cups in a broken-off oval 29 cm by 14 cm ($11\frac{1}{2}$ in × $5\frac{1}{2}$ in) and 5 cups. In two cases 2 cups are joined by a groove as a 'dumb-bell'.

Rock D – horizontal – has 2 cups-and-one-ring, 1 nearly weathered off, the other ungapped, with a radial groove from the cup.

Rock E – sloping 10°E – has 4 cups-and-one-gapped-ring, 2 with a radial groove from the cup. There is a curved groove enclosing one of these and another cup, and also 4 other cups, one in the groove.

Rock F – not visible in 1969–1976, probably now turfed over – 'on the summit rock' – 4 cups-and-one-incomplete-ring, 2 cups inside an oval with a third cup as 'runner' in the groove, 2 long grooves and 12 cups – scale unknown, but probably of similar size to the others listed above.

Rock G – not shown on the plan, and NW of the others – bears 1 cupmark.

Most of the carvings are much weathered. Greatest ring diameter 14 cm (5½ in) and carving depths up to 2 cm (1 in).

GRANGE — the site, looking N.W.

GRANGE — N.W. carved rock, looking S.

GAL 61   HIGH AUCHENLARIE 1

Coles 1894, p. 90
K. Inventory 1914, no.
  19
Morris & Bailey 1964,
  p. 162
Morris 1966, p. 108

Small outcrop 270 m NE of the farm, 5 km SW of Anwoth, 1¼ km inland, sea views from near, in rough grass. First reported by F. R. Coles (1894).

NX 5396 5339 OS: old 80 and Kirkcudbright 47 SE; new 83 and NX 55 SW. 145 m (475 ft).

16½ m (55 ft) SW of the SW stone now standing in the stone circle, is a hard-to-find wedge-shaped greywacke face 2 m by ⅔ m, 8 cm at its highest but sometimes turf-covered (6 ft × 2 ft × ¼ ft), sloping 20°SE. On it are –

A cup-and-two complete-rings with a radial groove from its cup to another cup outside, a cup-and-incomplete-ring, the ring ending in another cup, and 7 cups, one with a 'tail'. All being much weathered, the exact description has varied slightly in each earlier account, depending perhaps on the direction of the lighting, when seen.

HIGH AUCHENLARIE 1 — the carvings chalked in, as they existed in 1972.

HIGH AUCHENLARIE 1 — looking S.W.

HIGH AUCHENLARIE 2

Slab 'found on the farm', situated as last above. First reported by Sir James Simpson (1864).

NX 537 531 OS: same sheets as above.

Found when trenching waste land, kept for many years at Cardroness House, Anworth, and now in the display shed at Kirkdale House, there (NX 515 533), is a possible cist-cover (greywacke) 1 m by 1 m by 15 cm ($3\frac{1}{4}$ ft × 3 ft × $\frac{1}{2}$ ft). On its flat surface, partly flaked off, there remain –

A cup-and-six-gapped-rings with 2 parallel grooves from the cup, 40 cm ($15\frac{1}{2}$ in) diameter, a cup-and-three-half-rings with 6 cups inside the inner ring (the other halves possibly flaked off), 9 other sets of rings, only 6 having a central cup, and 4 being double rings, some rings complete, most being gapped, some with one, or two, radial grooves (some 'keyhole-type'), 12 other cups and some grooves. This slab seems to combine nearly all the motifs found commonly in the British Isles except the lozenge and the spiral. It is good that it is in 'protective custody', under cover.

Simpson 1864, p. 30, plate XIII
Simpson 1867, p. 32, plate XIII
Coles 1894, p. 91
Breuil 1934, p. 316
Truckell 1961, p. 192
Morris & Bailey 1964, p. 161
Morris 1966, p. 108
Simpson & Thawley 1972, pp. 101 & 90

HIGH AUCHENLARIE 2 — left, in natural light and right, with carvings chalked in. There are here probably the best assortment of designs found on such a slab in Scotland.

Outcrop ridge 400 m SE of the farm, 3 km SE of Kirkcudbright, 2½ km inland, sea views, in pasture. First reported by G. Hamilton (1886).

Hamilton 1886, p. 157
Hamilton 1888, p. 125
Coles 1894, p. 81
K. Inventory 1914, no.
 240
Feachem 1963, p. 91
Morris & Bailey 1964,
 p. 166
Morris 1966, p. 108

NX 709 489 OS: old 81 and Kirkcudbright 55 SW; new 84 and NX 74 NW. 115 m (380 ft).

On a rocky hillock in a field, 36 m (40 yds) NE of a wall, 108 m (120 yds) WNW of another wall, is an arched greywacke outcrop ridge, partly covered in deep turf, running NNE–SSW and sloping in various directions from 0° to 30°, but mostly horizontal where carved. On an area there of about 30 m by 1½ m and up to 14¼ m high (100 ft × 5 ft × 4 ft) but mostly at ground level and in line NNE–SSW, are one of the best collections of cup-and-ring carvings in Galloway. These include –

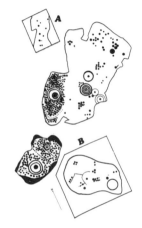

HIGHBANKS —The main area, uncovered in 1964–78, with the area marked "B". Also noted by Hamilton but turfed over of recent times, and the area marked "A" to the extreme N.E. of all carvings previously noted, first noted by the author in 1974.

(a) At the SSW end, well-preserved – at least 16 cups with up to 4 concentric rings, all un-gapped except where broken at the rock's edge, a ring with no observable central cup, at least 350 cups, many closely packed and in patterns, and also some man-made and natural grooves. There follows a gap of 8 m (9 yds). Then –

(b) At the NNE end, much weathered – at least 10 cups with up to 4 concentric rings, many now incomplete, and at least 26 cups.

(c) Out of line – 2 m (2 yds) to the W, near the SSW end of this last group is a cup-and two-now-incomplete-rings. And about half-way between the two main groups, but 3 m (yds) to the W, is a cup-and-six-complete-rings, surrounded by at least 13 much-weathered cups.

The greatest ring diameter occurs in group (a) – 45 cm (18 in) Carving depths are up to 5 cm (2 in). The two figures in group (c) are marked 'A' and 'B' in the accompanying sketch.

HIGH BANKS — the N.E. part found by F. R. Coles and now turf-covered. The carving marked "L" is 1 mile N.E. of the N.E.-most carvings on the other diagram. (After F. R. Coles' sketch). Scale 1:75.

HIGH BANKS — the main carvings, looking S.W. Photo by I. F. Macleod.

GAL 64　　　　　　　　　　HOWWELL 1

Hamilton 1886, p. 153
*　('Drumore')*
Coles 1894, p. 78
*　('Milton Park')*
Coles' sketches
*　('Dunrod')*
K. Inventory 1914, no.
*　241 ('Milton Park')*
Morris & Bailey 1964,
*　p. 166 ('Howell 4')*
Morris 1966, p. 108
*　('Howell 4')*

Outcrop 1000 m NE of Howwell farm, 6 km SE of Kirkcudbright, 2 km inland, sea views, in pasture. First reported by G. Hamilton (1886).

NX 7032 4575 OS: old 81 and Kirkcudbright 55 SW; new 84 and NX 74 NW. 65 m (220 ft).

1 m (yd) W of a high field wall 40 m (45 yds) N of its gate, in the field formerly called 'West Milton Park' within the Army's Heavy Weapons Practice Range, is a fairly smooth greywacke outcrop at ground level $1\frac{1}{2}$ m by $1\frac{1}{4}$ m (5 ft × 4 ft) sloping with the ground 20°NW. On it are –

At least 9 cups-and-rings (from 1 to 3 concentric rings), and 5 cups. Some rings are incomplete and one figure has a radial groove from a cup in its outer ring to the rock's edge. Earlier writers show some as ending in 2 parallel radial grooves ('keyhole-type'), but these may have weathered off. Greatest ring diameter 21 cm (8 in) and carving depths up to $\frac{1}{2}$ cm ($\frac{1}{4}$ in).

ARMY PERMISSION MUST BE OBTAINED BEFORE VISITING THIS SITE – PRACTICE SHELLING MAY BEGIN AT ANY TIME.

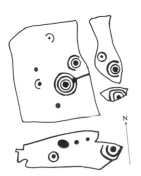

HOWWELL 1 — Scale 3:100.

HOWWELL 1 — with most of the figures chalked in, looking E.

HOWWELL 2　　　　　　　GAL 65

Small outcrop 80 m NE of GAL 64; in same situation as GAL 64. First reported by F. R. Coles (1894).

NX 703 457 OS: same sheets and altitude as GAL 64.

Coles 1894, p. 78
K. Inventory 1914, no. 241
Morris & Bailey 1964, p. 166
Morris 1966, p. 108

In the adjoining field, formerly called East Milton Park, on the Army's Heavy Weapons Practice Range, at the E end of one of several rocky areas, and about 110 m (120 yds) S by W of **GAL 67**, is a small greywacke outcrop, rather hard to find, 30 cm square (1 ft × 1 ft) just above ground level, sloping 10°E. On it are –

2 much-weathered cups-and-one-complete-ring 10 cm (4 in) diameter and 2 cups. Greatest carving depth $\frac{1}{2}$ cm ($\frac{1}{4}$ in).

Perhaps this is the same rocky area as that on which Coles described his find of '2 very much worn rings 4 and 7 in (10 and 18 cm) wide and a shallow cup', and the Royal Commission on Ancient Monuments of Scotland noted '1 small central cup, surrounded by three rings', with 4 or 5 small depressions beside it.

ARMY PERMISSION MUST BE OBTAINED BEFORE VISITING THIS SITE AS PRACTICE SHELLING MAY BEGIN AT ANY TIME.

HOWWELL 2 — a hard-to-find little outcrop, looking S.W.

GAL 66   HOWWELL 3

Hamilton 1886 p. 153
Coles 1894, p. 77
Coles' sketches
  ('Dunrod')
Morris & Bailey 1964,
  p. 166
Morris 1966, p. 108

Outcrop about 180 m NE of GAL 64, in same field and situation as GAL 65. First reported by G. Hamilton (1886).

NX 702 458 OS: same sheets and altitude as GAL 64.

Said to be roughly in the position given above, but not found either by the Royal Commission on Ancient Monuments of Scotland or the author and others, in recent times – probably turf-covered – is a finely carved outcrop sheet sloping 30°SE. On it are –

11 cups-and-rings, having from one to 5 concentric rings, some gapped, some complete, some incomplete, at least 2 cups, 2 oval depressions, and some connecting grooves.

AS WITH THE OTHERS HERE, ARMY PERMISSION MUST BE OBTAINED BEFORE SEARCHING FOR THIS SITE AS PRACTICE SHELLING MAY BEGIN AT ANY TIME.

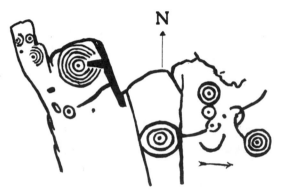

HOWWELL 3 — F. R. Coles' sketch of the carvings, now probably turfed over. It differs slightly from G. Hamilton's earlier sketch. (scale unknown).

GAL 67   HOWWELL 4

Outcrop 1200 m NE of Howwell farm, in same situation as GAL 64. First reported by F. R. Coles (1894).

NX 7041 4594 OS: Same sheets and altitude as GAL 64.

180 m (200 yds) S by E of the hay shed formerly 'Low Milton' and 150 m (160 yds) SW of the junction of the roads to Balig Hill and Silver Hill, in the same field as **GAL 65**, is a fairly prominent grey-

wacke outcrop $2\frac{3}{4}$ m by $2\frac{1}{2}$ m, $1\frac{1}{4}$ m high on its SW, at turf level, and practically invisible, from the NE (9 ft × 8 ft × 4 ft). On its smooth horizontal top are –

A cup-and-four-complete-rings 28 cm (11 in) diameter, with a radial groove from an inner ring and a cup as 'runner' in the outer rings, a cup-and-one-complete-ring tangental to it, a cup-and-two-incomplete-rings and, on an adjoining slab $\frac{3}{4}$ m (2 ft) NNW, a cup. Greatest carving depth 1 cm ($\frac{1}{2}$ in).

ARMY PERMISSION MUST BE OBTAINED BEFORE VISITING THIS SITE AS PRACTICE SHELLING MAY BEGIN AT ANY TIME.

Coles 1894, p. 78
K. Inventory 1914, no. 241
Coles' sketches ('Dunrod')
Morris & Bailey 1964, p. 166 ('Howwell 1')
Morris 1966, p. 108

HOWWELL 4 — the carvings chalked in.

HOWWELL 4 — looking W. the carving nearest the camera, sloping towards the viewer, does not show here.

GAL 68

HOWWELL 5

Coles 1894, p. 78

Outcrop in the Milton area, probably in the same situation as GAL 64.

NX 70 45 OS: Same sheets and approximate altitude as GAL 64.

In the Milton area Coles also noted a rock 'jutting up some 4 ft ($1\frac{1}{4}$ m) in the grass. On it was –

A cup surrounded by a near-semicircular groove $7\frac{1}{2}$ cm (3 in) diameter.

This has not been found by later searchers and may well have flaked off or become turf-covered.

When the Army Heavy Weapons Practice Range closes down a thorough search of these Milton fields would be worth while.

KIRKCLAUGH

Small slab in the farm's stable wall, 6 km SW of Anwoth, 6 km inland. First reported by F. R. Coles (1898).

NX 537 524 OS: old 80 and Kirkcudbright 53 NE; new 83 and NX 55 SW. 75 m (250 ft).

Built into the inside of the N wall of the washing shed at the stables, just below the roof, was a red sandstone slab 40 cm by 17 cm (15 in × 7 in). The shed has been partly re-built, and in 1964–76 the author has been unable to trace the slab. On it were –

11 cups, 2 cups-and-two-rings, and 3 cups-and-one-ring, all rings gapped, and with radial and other grooves, connecting all the carvings. Greatest ring diameter is 13 cm (5 in).

Coles 1898, p. 369
K. Inventory 1914, no. 23
Truckell 1961, p. 192
Morris & Bailey 1964, p. 163
Morris 1966, p. 110

KIRKCLAUGH — a rubbing taken of this now missing slab — by kind permission of the Royal Commission on Ancient Monuments of Scotland.

GAL 70   KIRKCUDBRIGHT MUSEUM

*Morris & Bailey 1964,
p. 172*
Morris 1966, p. 110

This well-arranged museum, in the centre of Kirkcudbright, houses the stones GAL 14 and 78 – Blackmyre and Laggan 1 – and also casts of GAL 63 – High Banks – and the late F. R. Coles' plans of a number of other sites.

GAL 71   KIRKDALE HOUSE

NX 515 533 OS: old 80 and Kirkcudbright 47 SW; new 83 and NX 55 SW.

*K. Inventory 1914, no.
20*
Truckell 1961, p. 192
Feachem 1963, p. 104
*Morris & Bailey 1964,
p. 162*
Morris 1966, p. 104

In a specially built open shed at the W end of the lawn behind the house, the owner has cemented in 6 cup-and-ring-carved stones and 2 Early Christian Crosses, all found on the former large estate of Cardroness, and some of which were formerly kept at Cardroness House. These include one stone whose exact provenance is unknown –

Greywacke slab 70 cm by 40 cm by 6 cm ($2\frac{1}{4}$ ft $\times$ $1\frac{1}{2}$ ft $\times$ $\frac{1}{4}$ ft). On its fairly smooth surface is –

A cup-and-five-complete-rings with a very small part of a sixth ring, and a shallow radial groove, probably from the inner ring only, to the stone's edge. The rings are not very circular. Greatest diameter 36 cm (14 in) and carving depths up to $\frac{1}{2}$ cm ($\frac{1}{4}$ in).

The others in the shed are –

GAL 12 – Barholm 1.
GAL 62 – High Auchenlarie 2.
GAL 79 – Laggan 2.
GAL 80 – Laggan 3.
GAL 110 – Upper Newton.

KIRKLDALE HOUSE — one of the stones in the shed — of unknown provenance except that it was found on Cardroness estate, and for many years was built into a sun-dial.

Outcrop 100 m SE of the farm, 2½ km SSE of Creetown, ½ km inland, sea views; in pasture. First reported by J. Flett (1926).

Flett 1926, p. 140–143
Morris & Bailey 1964, p. 163
Morris 1966, p. 110

NX 483 562 OS: old 80 and Kirkcudbright 47 NW; new 83 and NX 45 NE. 90 m (300 ft).

In 'Wee Eric's Field', 32 m (35 yds) S of the lower field's gate, 15 m (17 yds) E of a wall, is a greywacke outcrop exposed in 1967–72 for 3½ m by 1 m (12 ft × 3 ft) at ground level, sloping 3°W. On its smooth surface (covered now by a few inches of soil for preservation) were –

7 cups-and-complete-rings, having from 1 to 5 rings, up to 27 cm (10½ in) diameter, all very lightly pocked and with very small central cups – all of negligible depths. By 1972 the 2 southmost had weathered off, hence the author's re-covering of this site, to preserve the rest.

27 m (30 yds) NW, in the corner beside 2 wall junctions, is a cup 7 cm (3 in) diameter, 5 cm (2 in) deep. 20 m (22 yds) E, near the hilltop, there are at least 5 well-defined cups.

KIRKMABRECK — the site, looking S.W. — to the right of the hay-rack.

KIRKMABRECK — looking S. A small carving is out of the picture at the top, and 2 further to the right appeared in 1974, to have completely weathered off.

KIRKMABRECK — the cup-marks on top of the hillock on the right of the site picture.

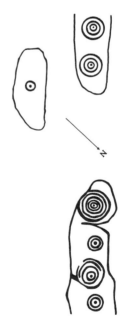

KIRKMABRECK — Scale 3:100.

GAL 73~74   KIRKMUIR 1~2

Coles 1905, p. 326
K. Inventory 1914, no.
  294
Morris & Bailey 1964,
  p. 163
Morris 1966, p. 110
Mann 1915, pp. 12 and
  15

2 outcrops 180 m E of the ruined Kirkdale Church, 7 km WSW of Anwoth, 1 km inland, sea views, in rough grass. First reported by F. R. Coles (1905).

NX 513 541 and 5137 5411 OS: old 80 and Kirkcudbright 47 SW; new 83 and NX 55 SW. 150 m (490 ft).

GAL 73 – 9 m (30 ft) W of the wall running up the hill was an outcrop with an almost level surface. It has now either been blasted away or deeply covered with earth. On it, besides 2 natural hollows, were –

A cup-and-complete-ring with a radial groove outwards from the ring, 10 cm (4 in) diameter and 14 cups, 2 of which are connected by a groove.

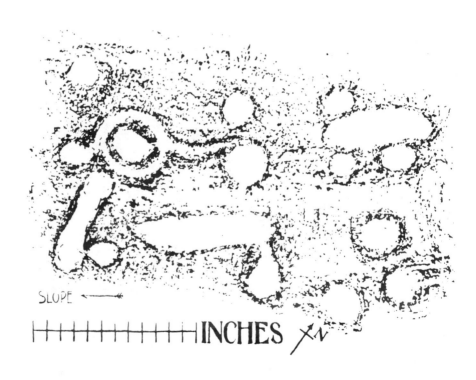

KIRKMUIR 1 — A rubbing made by the Royal Commission on Ancient Monuments of Scotland of this carving, now missing. Reproduced by their kind permission.

KIRKMUIR 2 — The rock recently found by the Ordnance Survey Archaeology Division — looking W. towards the old graveyard of Kirkmuir.

KIRKMUIR 2 — The same stone, showing some of the rather faint carvings, looking W.

GAL 74 – 'Immediately across the wall to the Eastwards, Coles noted another outcrop, now also either blasted or deeply covered. On it were –

At least 6 cups-and-gapped-rings with radial grooves from their cups, 2 with two rings, the others with 1. There is a rudimentary design in the lay-out of these carvings. Greatest diameter – 16 cm ($6\frac{1}{2}$ in).

On a greywacke outcrop ridge 100 m (110 yds) S of a field wall, 11 m (12 yds) E of another wall, about 2 m by 1 m, $\frac{1}{4}$ m high ($6\frac{1}{2}$ ft × 3 ft × 1 ft), the Ordnance Survey, Archaeology Division, recently found 14 cup-marks up to $2\frac{1}{2}$ cm (1 in) deep, one surrounded by a possible, but very faint, ring 10 cm (4 in) diameter. Excavation of the same ridge further E, where now turfed over, may possibly reveal the carvings noted by Coles.

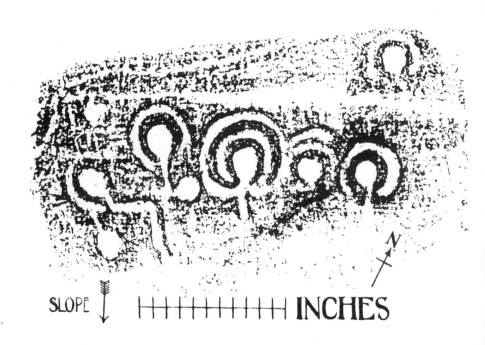

KIRKMUIR 2 — Another of the Commission's rubbings, reproduced by their kind permission, of this stone, also now missing.

KNOCK 1 GAL 75

Outcrop ledge 900 m W of Low Knock, 4 km SE of Port William, ⅛ km inland, sea views, in rough grass. First reported by F. R. Coles (1905).

NX 364 401 OS: old 80 and Wigtown 30 SE; new 83 and NX 34 SE. 24 m (40 ft).

Coles 1905, p. 327
Ferguson 1961, p. 47 ('Monreith')
R. S. G. Anderson 1926, p. 121
McWhite 1964, p. 80
Morris & Bailey 1964, p. 170
Morris 1966, p. 110

There is a cattle grid on the road to Kirkmaiden. Beyond it a wall on the seaward side of the road turns a right angle towards the sea. 55 m (60 yds) WSW of this corner is a rocky hillock on the clifftop. On it is a greywacke mass about 15 m by 3 m (50 ft × 10 ft), up to 3 m (10 ft) high. On a small ledge on its E side, about 1 m (3 ft) above the ground sloping 10° SW are –

A four-convolution single spiral 17 cm (7 in) diameter and a 'grid' comprising 6 near-rectangular compartments, 16 cm by 13 cm (6 in × 5 in). Greatest carving depth about ¼ cm. (⅛ in). The grid, at least, seems to have been incised, not the usual pocking, and could be a more recent addition.

There are a number of cup-marked rocks in the vicinity of Knock, including 2, 10 m (11 yds) to the N and to the SE.

KNOCK 1 — the site, looking N.E. The car is at the cattle grid mentioned opposite.

KNOCK 1 — the rectangles and spiral.

KNOCK 1 — the carvings chalked in.

KNOCK 2

GAL 76

Outcrop 1 km WNW of Low Knock, 4 km SE of Port William, $\frac{1}{4}$ km inland, sea views, in pasture. First reported by the Royal Commission on Ancient Monuments of Scotland (1911).

NX 364 405 OS: same sheets and altitude as GAL 75.

K. Inventory 1914, no. 14
Morris & Bailey 1964, p. 170
Morris 1966, p. 110

About 23 m (25 yds) E of Clarksburn Woods E wall, 118 m (130 yds) S of the road A747 is a rough, uncultivated raised area. Near its NE end, in 1965, on a surface sloping 15°S, was a just-discernable cup-and-two-complete-rings; and a similar one, partly flaked off, was on the area's W side, near the bottom, on a surface sloping 25°N, – both figures 18 cm (7 in) diameter and of negligible depth. Since 1970 the author has searched several times for these but has been unable to find either.

Mr. Lamber, 'Knockbrae', states that, after blasting, these are now in the stone-heap mentioned below.

KNOCK 3

GAL 76a

2 outcrops 1 km WNW of Low Knock, $\frac{1}{2}$ km inland, sea views, in pasture. First reported by C. Jackson (1978).

NX 365 406 OS: same sheets and altitude as GAL 75.

17 m (19 yds) E of road A747, opposite 'Knockbrae', 127 m (140 yds) E of Clarksburn wood's wall, in same field as last, 9 m (10 yds) E of a stone-heap, is a greywacke outcropping area with turf. On it are 2 carved areas –

(a) An area $1\frac{1}{2}$ m by $\frac{3}{4}$ m ($2\frac{1}{2}$ ft × $1\frac{1}{4}$ ft) at ground level, sloping 10°N. On it are –

3 irregularly-shaped partly weathered-off ovaloid cups-and-rings up to 23 cm (9 in) diameters, $\frac{1}{4}$ cm $\frac{1}{8}$ in) deep, 2 with 2 rings, 1 with 3.

(b) $6\frac{1}{2}$ m (7 yds) S of this, on a triangular area 1 m (yd) each way at ground level, sloping 10°N, are –

Parts of 3 much weathered cups-and-two-rings 12 cm (5 in) diameters, $\frac{1}{4}$ cm ($\frac{1}{8}$ in) deep.

KNOCK 3 — the two newly-discovered carvings are marked by a white can on the left and a ranging rod on the right. The carved stones, Knock 2, are believed now to be in the rubble behind this site.

KNOCK 3 — the group nearest the main road, looking E.

KNOCK 3 — the group farthest from the road, looking E.

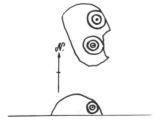

KNOCK 3 — group nearest the main road. Scale 3:100.

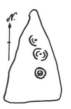

KNOCK 3 — grop farest from the road. Scale 3:100.

Outcrop 1 km WNW of Low Knock, $\frac{1}{4}$ km inland, sea views, in pasture. First reported by C. Jackson (1978).

NX 364 405 OS: same sheets and altitude as GAL 75.

158 m (173 yds) S of road A747, 1 m (yd) E of Clarksburn Wood's wall, is a smooth outcrop or sunk boulder $1\frac{1}{4}$ m by $1\frac{1}{4}$ m, up to 10 cm high (4 ft × 4 ft × $\frac{1}{4}$ ft) sloping 5° SSE. On it are –

A cup-and-four-complete-rings 28 cm by 24 cm (11 in × $9\frac{1}{2}$ in) and at least 10 cups, some of which have faint traces of rings. Greatest carving depths – $\frac{1}{2}$ cm ($\frac{1}{4}$ in).

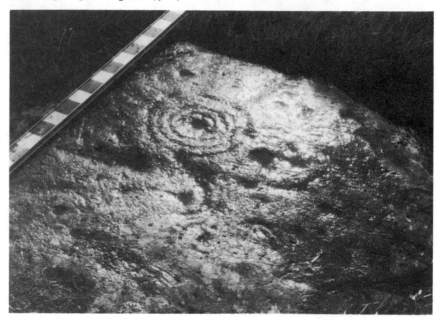

KNOCK 4 — the carvings on this table-like flat rock-looking E.

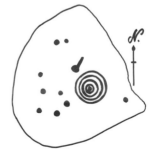

KNOCK 4 — the carved rock is in the foreground — looking W.   KNOCK 4 — Scale 3:100.

KNOCKSHINNIE

Outcrop 470 m ESE of Torrs farm, 5 km S of Kirkcudbright, 1¼ km inland, sea views, on moor. First reported by G. Hamilton (1886).

NX 6844 4555 OS: old 80 and Kirkcudbright 58 NW; new 83 and NX 64 NE. 110 m (370 ft).

6 m (7 yds) SE of a wall, 57 m (63 yds) S of its corner with another wall, is a smooth gritstone outcrop, partly turf-striped, 4½ m by 3½ m, up to ½ m high (15 ft × 12 ft × 1½ ft), mostly sloping 10°E. On it, all much weathered, are –

A cup-and-four-irregular-rings or part-rings, with a cup as 'runner', an incomplete cup-and-two-rings, 2 cups-and-one-ring (1 gapped) and at least 13 cups. Several of these figures are joined by radial and other grooves, including a partly natural one joining 6 of them in an almost N/S line. Greatest diameter 37 cm (14½ in) and carving depths up to 3 cm (1 in).

Mr. Picken, (owner) states there are 2 other cup-and-ring stones, now covered in dense gorse – (a) about 350 m (400 yds) S of the site, and (b) over the wall, about 90 m (100 yds) W of it.

*Hamilton 1886, p. 155
('Dromore')
Coles 1894, p. 72
K. Inventory 1914, no. 247
Morris & Bailey 1964, p. 168 ('Torrs 6')
Morris 1966, p. 114 (do.)*

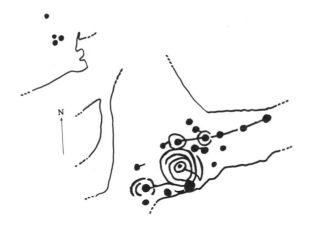

KNOCKSHINNIE — scale 3:100.

KNOCKSHINNIE — looking S.W.

GAL 78   LAGGAN 1

*Truckell 1961, p. 194,
fig. 8
Morris & Bailey 1964,
p. 163
Morris 1966, p. 110*

Small slab found 'on the farm', now in Kirkcudbright Museum. First reported by Mr. Sproat (1961).

NX 54 53 OS: old 80, new 83.

A greywacke slab 46 cm by 23 cm, 5 cm thick ($1\frac{1}{2}$ ft $\times \frac{3}{4}$ ft $\times \frac{1}{4}$ ft) was found in the bed of a shallow stream and brought to the museum. On its smooth surface is –

    A cup-and-seven-rings and a cup-and-two-rings, all rings un-gapped except where broken by the stone's edge. There are 2 radial grooves outwards from a ring, 1 of which may be natural. The carvings here are very like those on the other 'portable' slab **GAL 26 – Cairnholy 1.**

LAGGAN 1 — this stone, found on the farm, is now in Kirkcudbright Museum.

GAL 79   LAGGAN 2

*Coles 1894, p. 189
K. Inventory 1914, no.
20
Feachem 1963, p. 91
Morris & Bailey 1964,
p. 163
Truckell 1961, p. 192
Morris 1966, p. 110*

Slab – possible cist-cover – found 'on the farm', now at Kirkdale House – GAL 71. First reported by F. R. Coles (1894).

NX 545 524 OS: old 80, new 83. 5 km SW of Anwoth, $\frac{3}{4}$ km inland. 35 m (120 ft).

A fairly smooth greywacke slab 1 m by $\frac{3}{4}$ m by 15 cm (3 ft $\times 2\frac{1}{2}$ ft $\times \frac{1}{2}$ ft) was found 'near the base of Laggan Hill, almost exactly 600 m (660 yds) WSW of the 'Four Standing Stones of Newton' on a 'thorny whin-grown slope' and taken to Cardroness House, and recently moved to Kirkdale House. On it are –

    3 cups-and-gapped-rings, each with 2 parallel radial grooves from the cup ('keyhole-type'), 2 with 4 rings and 1 with 5. Greatest diameter – 24 cm ($9\frac{1}{2}$ in) and carving depths up to $\frac{1}{2}$ cm ($\frac{1}{4}$ in).

LAGGAN 2 — this stone, found on the farm, is now at Kirkdale House. It, just possibly, was part of a cist.

LAGGAN 3   GAL 80

Small slab, 'found on the farm', 7 km SW of Anwoth, $\frac{3}{4}$ km inland, now at Kirkdale House, Anwoth. First reported by A. E. Truckell (1961).

Truckell 1961, p. 194
Morris & Bailey 1964,
  p. 163
Morris 1966, p. 110

NX 520 537 OS: old 80 and Kirkcudbright 47 SW; new 83 and NX 55 SW. 110 m (360 ft).

Found in the wall running up the E side of Kirkdale burn, almost opposite **Cairnholy 1 – GAL 26** – was a flat slab $\frac{1}{2}$ m by $\frac{1}{4}$ m by $\frac{1}{8}$ m ($1\frac{1}{2}$ ft × $\frac{3}{4}$ ft × $\frac{1}{2}$ ft), now in the shed at Kirkdale House – **GAL 71** – a cast of which is in the National Museum of Antiquities, no IA 42. On it is –

A broken-off cup-and-four-complete-rings with a small part of a fifth ring, 20 cm ($7\frac{1}{2}$ in) diameter. There is a radial groove, deeper than the rings, so making them appear 'gapped' in some lights. It runs from the cup to the stone's edge. Deepest carving – $\frac{1}{2}$ cm ($\frac{1}{4}$ in).

135

LAGGAN 3 — This, also found on the farm, is now at Kirkdale House.

GAL 81 LAGGAN MULLAN

K. *Inventory 1914, no.*
24
Morris & Bailey 1964,
p. 163
Morris 1966, p. 110

Outcrop 100 m S of the farm, 1¾ km WSW of Anwoth, ¾ km inland, open to the S; in rough grass. First reported by the Royal Commission on Ancient Monuments of Scotland (1912).

NX 5650 5518 OS: old 80 and Kirkcudbright 47 SE; new 83 and NX 55 NE. 53 m 175 ft).

'At the edge of the field and on the E side of its wall and some 40 ft (12 m) up from the gate' is said to be –

'A group of rock sculpturings from time to time exposed in ploughing'. Although noted by the Royal Commission as existing on their visit in 1912 it was then covered, and between 1964 and 1978 it has not been uncovered and is unknown to the farmer.

LAMFORD 1~2 GAL 82~83

2 outcrops 1500 m ESE of the farm, 6½ km NW of Carsphairn, 28 km inland, wide loch views, on moor. First reported by M. F. Ansell (1966).

Morris & Bailey 1964, p. 168.
Morris 1966, p. 110

NX 5513 9888 OS: old 67 and Kirkcudbright 3; new 77 and NX 59 NW. 305 m (1000 ft).

GAL 82 – 18 m (20 yds) E of a stone sheepfold's NE end, among other rocks is a pillar-like greywacke outcrop 1¼ m by 1 m, and 1 m high (4 ft × 3 ft × 3 ft). On its horizontal top are –

2 cups-and-one-complete-ring, each 7½ cm (3 in) diameter, with rather big central cups 2 cm (¾ in) deep.

LAMFORD 1 — the carvings from above. They have similarities with the carving found in Glentrool. (GAL 59).

GAL 83 – 27 m (30 yds) SE of this is another outcrop. It slopes 30°SW, is rather triangular, 3½ m by 3 m, 1¼ m high on its SE, at ground level elsewhere (12 ft × 10 ft × 4 ft). On its fairly smooth face are –

4 cups-and-one-complete-ring 7½ cm (3 in) diameters, up to 2 cm (¾ in) deep.

There are a number of cup-marked rocks in this area, including those 23 m (25 yds) S, 60 m (65 yds) SE and 220 m (240 yds) SE.

This is the highest site in Galloway, so far known to the author, bearing cups-and-rings, and only **Duchrae – GAL 50** – which bears rings only, is further from the sea. This and the Duchrae sites lie on what was probably one of man's earliest routes from the Solway to the Clyde valley.

LAMFORD 2 — looking S.W.

LAMFORD 2 — the carvings chalked in.

LOW BANKS 1   GAL 84

Outcrop 900 m ESE of the farm, 4 km SE of Kirkcudbright, 3 km inland, sea views, in rough grass. First reported by the Royal Commission on Ancient Monuments of Scotland (1914).

NX 7058 4849 OS: old 81 and Kirkcudbright 55 SW; new 83 and NX 74 NW. 100 m (350 ft).

K. Inventory 1914, no. 250 (Galtway)
Morris & Bailey 1964, p. 167
Morris 1966, p. 112

About 190 m (210 yds) SE of Galtway churchyard's SE wall, 137 m (150 yds) SW of the field's wall, was a hard-to-find quartz-veined greywacke outcrop $1\frac{3}{4}$ m by $1\frac{3}{4}$ m, (6 ft × 6 ft) at ground level, sloping 5° W. On it is –

A much-weathered cup-and-one-complete-ring 15 cm (6 in) diameter and a cup, 1 cm. ($\frac{1}{2}$ in) deep. 3 other carvings were found in this vicinity by the Royal Commission, but could not be traced by the author and may have weathered off. This site has now become turf-covered and untraceable.

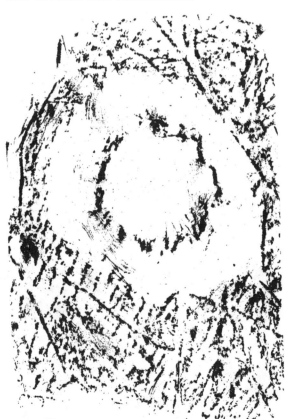

LOW BANKS 1 — a rubbing of this carving, now lost once more under the turf.

Coles 1894, p. 79
(Galtway)
K. Inventory 1914, no.
251 (Galtway)
Morris & Bailey 1964,
p. 167
Morris 1966, p. 112

Outcrop 900 m E of the farm, 4 km SE of Kirkcudbright, 3 km inland, sea views, in rough grass. First reported by F. R. Coles (1894).

NX 7070 4878 OS: same sheets and altitude as last above.

In the field NE of the last above, 100 m (110 yds) SE of its wall, 155 m (170 yds) NE of another wall, is a low outcropping turf ridge. On it 2 nearly adjoining small horizontal greywacke outcrops at ground level, 1 m by $\frac{3}{4}$ m (3 ft × $2\frac{1}{4}$ ft) and $\frac{1}{3}$ m (1 ft) square, have –

A cup-and-four rings a semi-circle, and a cup-and-three-rings. Some rings are complete, others weathered off or partial. Greatest diameter 15 cm (6 in) and carving depths up to 1 cm ($\frac{1}{2}$ in).

It seems possible that these sites on Low Banks farm may be parts of one or other of the sites listed as 'Galtway' – **GAL 53–56** – although the carvings found there previously seem different.

LOW BANKS 2 — looking S.S.W. towards the sea. The site is marked by the ranging rod.

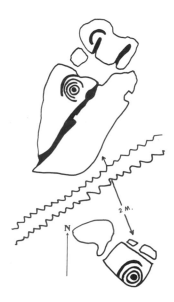

LOW BANKS 2 — Scale 3:100.

LOW BANKS 2 — the much-weathered S.E. rock, looking S.

LOW BANKS 2 — the N.W. rock, looking S.

GAL 86 LOWER LAGGAN COTTAGE

Slab, found elsewhere, now missing, once in the garden, 5 km SW of Anwoth. First reported by the Royal Commission on Ancient Monuments (1914).

K. Inventory 1914, no. 22
Truckell 1961, p. 192
Feachem 1963, p. 91
Morris & Bailey 1964, p. 163
Morris 1966, p. 112

NX 545 526 OS: old 80 and 54 NE; new 83 and NX 55 SW.

Greywacke slab $\frac{2}{3}$ m by $\frac{1}{2}$ m (2 ft × 1$\frac{1}{2}$ ft) and thin, broken into 3 pieces, once built into a wall somewhere on Upper Laggan Hill, then kept in this garden, on S side of road A75, NE of the road to Mossyard, now missing, possibly taken by last occupier before 1965. On it were –

12 cups-and-one-complete-ring and 5 cups. The cups were bigger than average, and the rings were very close round them – as with **GAL 110**, and were mostly connected by grooves from the cups.

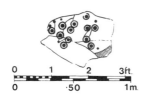

0   1   2   3 ft.

0   ·50   1 m.

LOWER LAGGAN COTTAGE — the broken slab, now missing, pieced together. Photograph by A. E. Truckell.

MILTON 1

2 adjoining outcrops found on the farm 'N of Low Milton', about 600 m S of farm, 5 km, SE of Kirkcudbright, 2½ km inland, in rough grass, sea views. First reported by F. R. Coles (1894).

Coles 1894, p. 78
K. Inventory 1914, no. 242
Morris & Bailey 1964, p. 167
Morris 1966, p. 112

NX 704 462 OS: old 81 and 55 SW; new 83 and NX 74 NW. 85 m (280 ft).

'Low Milton' is now a ruined hayshed on the S side of the road. The 2 outcrops have been untraceable since at least 1911 and probably are turf-covered. In 1894 Coles found them, 'each face W and in each the cups lie due E and W'. On the 2 respectively were –

(a) 2 cups-and-complete-rings, 1 with 2 and the other with 3, rings and part of a fourth. No measurements or scale are given.

(b) 2 cups-and-one-complete-ring, joined by a slightly V-shaped groove, and a cup. No measurements or scale are given.

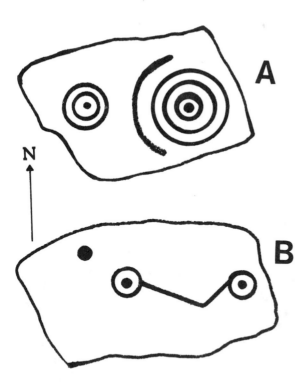

MILTON 1 — the 2 slabs, after F. R. Coles' sketches. Scale unknown. Neither slab can be traced at present.

GAL 88   MILTON 2

Morris & Bailey 1964 p. 167
Morris 1966, p. 112

Outcrop 500 m SE of farm, 5 km SE of Kirkcudbright, $2\frac{3}{4}$ km inland, sea views, in rough grass. First reported by the author (1964).

NX 708 463 OS: same sheets as last above. 100 m (330 ft).

In Upper Glen Field, 32 m (30 yds) from the NW wall's gate near its NE end, was a small greywacke outcrop 10 cm (4 in) below ground, now turfed over and un-traceable since 1964. On it, the farmer, Mr. Picken, reported to the author there were –

A cup-and-gapped-ring with 2 parallel grooves outward from the ring ('keyhole-type').

GAL 89   MILTON 3

Small outcrop 19 m W of 'the Bungalow', Milton, $4\frac{1}{2}$ km SE of Kirkcudbright, 3 km inland, sea views, in pasture. First noted by the author (1973).

NX 704 469 OS: same sheets as last two above. 100 m (330 ft).

Greywacke outcrop at ground level, uncovered in 1973 for 2 m by $1\frac{1}{4}$ m (7 ft × 4 ft). On a smooth part of it, sloping 5°NW, is –

A cup-and-three-complete-rings 22 cm ($8\frac{1}{2}$ in) diameter, and 3 cups – carving up to 1 cm ($\frac{1}{2}$ in) deep.

MILTON 3 — looking S.

MILTON 3 — looking S.

MILTON 3 — the carvings chalked in.

GAL 90   MOSSYARD 1

*K. Inventory 1914, no.
21*
Feachem 1963, p. 91
*Morris & Bailey 1964,
p. 163*
*Morris 1966, pp. 82 &
112*

Outcrop 600 m SW of the farm, 5¾ km SW of Anwoth, ¾ km inland, sea views, in pasture. First reported by the Royal Commission on Ancient Monuments of Scotland (1914).

NX 545 514 OS: old 80 and Kirkcudbright 53 NE; new 83 and NX 55 SW. 20 m (60 ft).

A few centimetres (in) NE of the wall along the steep shore, 145 m (160 yds) NW of another field wall, is a broken-up greywacke hump 4 m by 1 m, up to ½ m high (13 ft × 3½ ft × 2 ft), partly turf. On 2 fairly smooth areas about ¾ m (2½ ft) apart, both sloping 5°NE are 2 figures –

A cup-and-five-rings with a radial groove from the cup; and a cup-and-three-rings with a radial groove, apparently from an inner ring. Some rings seem gapped, others complete. There are also some probably natural grooves and cavities.

MOSSYARD 1 — the W cup-and-ring, looking W.

146

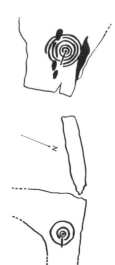

MOSSYARD 1 — Scale 3:100.

MOSSYARD 1 — the N.E. carving, first noted by the author, in 1972.

Small slab found on the farm, 5 km SW of Anwoth, now in the National Museum of Antiquities of Scotland, Edinburgh no IA 33. First reported by Sir Herbert R. Maxwell (1900).

Maxwell 1900 p. 151
Morris & Bailey 1964,
p. 164
Morris 1966, p. 112

NX 55 52 OS: same sheets as above.

In 1900 Sir Herbert R. Maxwell presented to the Society of Antiquaries of Scotland a greywacke slab which had been found built into a wall on the farm. It was $\frac{3}{4}$ m by $\frac{1}{3}$ m by 15 cm ($2\frac{1}{2}$ ft × 1 ft × $\frac{1}{2}$ ft). On its smooth surface were –

A cup-and-five-rings, the rings slightly flattened where a radial groove from the cup passes through them, 23 cm ($9\frac{1}{2}$ in) diameter, grooves connecting this with 3 other cups. Carving depths up to $\frac{1}{2}$ cm ($\frac{1}{4}$ in). The rings are rather lightly pecked though quite wide, and well preserved. All are gapped, except the inner ring.

MOSSYARD 2 — now in the National Museum of Antiquities of Scotland, Edinburgh.

MOSSYARD 3

GAL 91a

Outcrops 250 m NW of farm, 5 km SW of Anwoth, $\frac{3}{4}$ km inland, sea views, in pasture. First reported by the Archaeology Division, Ordnance Survey (1977).

NX 5470 5205. Same sheets as last above. 30 m (100 ft).

Near the road to the farm, 55 m (60 yds) S of a field gate, is a rocky area (greywacke), about 22 m by 12 m (24 yds × 14 yds), – a low hummock. Near its SW end are 4 slightly separated outcrops, horizontal or sloping up to 5°N to W, carved thus –

(a) A cup-and-four-complete-rings with two faint parallel radial grooves from the inner ring and one cup.

(b) 2 m NW of it – a cup-and-four-complete-rings, 2 cups-and-three-rings (both very faint) and 4 cups which may have had rings once.

(c) 1 m NW of 'B', 2 small cups-and-two-rings, 1 'keyhole-type' with central cup and its ring-ends turning outwards, and 1 with a radial groove from its cup.

(d) 2 m S of 'C', a 'keyhole-type' cup-and-one-ring with a radial groove from its cup parallel to the outward-turning ring ends, and 3 possible cups.

Greatest ring diameter (a) 27 cm ($10\frac{1}{2}$ in) and carving depths up to 1 cm ($\frac{1}{2}$ in).

MOSSYARD 3 — the S.E. carved slab, looking S.W.

Outcrops 195 m NE of the farm, 7½ km NE of Kirkcudbright, 6 km inland, open site, in rough grass. First reported by F. R. Coles (1894).

Coles 1894, p. 85–86
K. Inventory 1914, no. 420
Morris & Bailey 1964, p. 167
Morris 1966, p. 112

NX 750 546 OS: old 81 and Kirkcudbright 49 SE; new 84 and NX 75 SE. 145 m (475 ft).

14 m (15 yds) W of the field's E wall, in a rough wooded area, is a fairly prominent greywacke outcropping shelf, 5 m by 1 m, up to ¾ m high on its NW (17 ft × 3 ft × 2½ ft). 1 m to its NW is a greywacke boulder 2 m by 1 m, ⅓ m high (6½ ft × 3 ft × 1 ft). On these, in 1894 there were –

(a) On the outcrop shelf where sloping 30°NW, 10 cups-and-complete-rings, 1 with a radial groove from its cup and 1 with a tangential groove from the ring. Coles noted up to 4 concentric rings, and 1 was a possible 'start of a spiral'. In 1964–76, however, even when wet in low sun, all that could be traced was a cup-and-four-complete-rings with parts of a fifth ring and a cup-and-two-rings both practically weathered off.

(b) On the boulder, on horizontal surface, a cup-and-four-complete-rings with about 50 straight lines radiating outwards from the rings was noted – a practically unique design in Scotland. In 1964–76 none of these lines could be seen, but there is a faint cup-and-six-complete-rings. Greatest diameter – 41 cm (16 in), carving depths negligible.

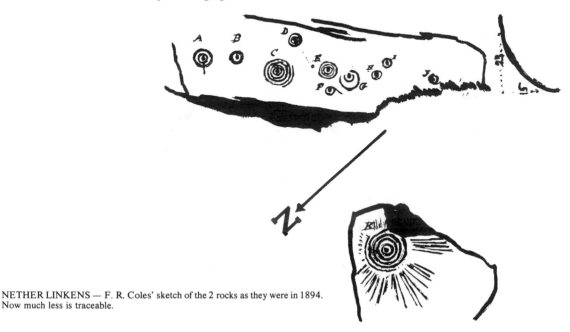

NETHER LINKENS — F. R. Coles' sketch of the 2 rocks as they were in 1894. Now much less is traceable.

NETHER LINKENS — The site, looking S.E. The faint carvings now remaining are in front of the ranging rod, and on the boulder at bottom R.

NETHER LINKENS — the biggest carving on the outcrop shelf. The other is on the R.

NETHER LINKENS — the carvings on the boulder, looking S. Once there were "rays" outwards from the rings.

GAL 93

NEWLAW BRIDGE

Coles 1894, p. 86
Morris & Bailey 1964,
   p. 167
Morris, 1966, p. 112

Slab built into the road bridge over the Newland Burn, now missing; 7 km ESE of Kirkcudbright. First reported by F. R. Coles (1894).

NX 742 470 OS: old 81 and Kirkcudbright 55 SE; new 83 and NX 74 NW. 90 m (300 ft).

Built in, as part of the top coping of the N side of the old bridge on road A711, Coles noted a long narrow slab. On it were –

8 concentric semi-circles with a central half-cup. There was a big gap between the 2 outer rings and the others. No scale or measurement is given. The bridge has been re-built, and the slab is now untraceable.

NEWLAW BRIDGE — F. R. Coles' sketch of this slab, built into the former road-bridge, and now missing. Scale unknown.

GAL 94

NEWLAW HILL 1

Coles 1898, p. 367
K. Inventory 1914, no.
   421
Morris & Bailey 1964,
   p. 167
Morris 1966, p. 112

Smooth outcrops 800 m SSW of Auchengool House, 5 km ESE of Kirkcudbright, 4 km inland, sea views, in rough grass. First reported by F. R. Coles (1898).

NX 7332 4887 OS: old 81 and Kirkcudbright 55 NE; new 83 and NX 74 NW. 145 m (475 ft).

400 m (450 yds) SSW of the road, on a line looking straight up Auchengool House's E avenue, 50 m (55 yds) WSW of some prominent hawthorn trees, 23 m (25 yds) SE of a spring, is a hard-to-find fragmented but smooth greywacke outcrop, sloping 15°NNW, $4\frac{1}{2}$ m by $1\frac{3}{4}$ m (15 ft × 6 ft) up to $\frac{1}{3}$ m (1 ft) high. On it are –

11 cups-and-rings, having up to 5 concentric rings, some of them gapped or incomplete, others complete, 2 with a radial groove from the cup, 1 with a groove from its outer ring, one central cup being 15 cm (6 in) diameter. There are also at least 53 cups, some of which are within the rings. Greatest ring diameter – 57 cm (22½ in) and carving depths up to 5 cm (2 in). The carvings are well preserved except where broken off. Some rings are far from circular and, in one case, 2 surround a natural 'hole'. Cole in 1894 thought this last was a 'volute' (or spiral), but it is now partly broken off and what is left seems more like parts of 2 oval rings.

NEWLAW HILL — the carvings, looking S.E.

NEWLAW HILL 1 — the site looking N. Auchengool House is in the trees on the left. Its avenue is in the distant centre.

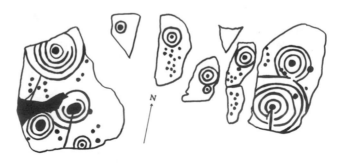

NEWLAW HILL   Scale 3:100.

154

NEWLAW HILL 2

GAL 95

Outcrop about 50 m SW of GAL 94, untraced by the author. First reported by F. R. Coles (1898).

Coles 1898, p. 367
K. Inventory 1914, no. 412
Morris & Bailey 1964, p. 167
Morris 1966, p. 112

NX 733 488 OS: same sheets and altitude as GAL 94.

Coles reported in 1898 that there was a cup-and-one-ring with a radial groove on a rock 90 m (100 yds) W of **GAL 94**.

The Royal Commission on Ancient Monuments for Scotland reported finding in 1911, some 50 or 60 yds (45 to 55 m) SW of **GAL 94** a much weathered cup-and-two-rings.

Just possibly these are the same carving, but neither could be traced by the author or other recent searchers, and they may be turfed over or weathered off.

NEWLAW HILL 3

GAL 96

Coles reported hearing that 'several hundred yards distant, higher up among the moors, there exists another group of scribings'. Coles was unable to locate these and, so far as the author knows, they have not since then been traced.

Coles 1898, p. 367
Morris & Bailey 1964, p. 167
Morris 1966, p. 112

NORTH BALFERN

GAL 97

Outcrop shelf 155 m WNW of the farm $4\frac{1}{2}$ km S of Wigtown, $1\frac{3}{4}$ km inland, sea views, in pasture. First reported by F. R. Coles (1902).

Coles 1902, p. 220–222
W. Inventory 1914, no. 220
Morris & Bailey 1964, p. 171
Feachem 1963, p. 93
Morris 1966, p. 112

NX 4337 5098 OS: old 80 and Wigtown 26 NE; new 83 and NX 45 SW. 30 m (100 ft).

In the field across the road from the farm, on the farthest of 3 rough areas, probably mostly turfed over (for preservation) is a greywacke outcrop, bared by the author temporarily for $2\frac{1}{2}$ m by 1 m, dropping vertically at its E $\frac{1}{4}$ m (9 ft × 3 ft × 1 ft), sloping 10°NE. On it, much weathered are –

19 cups-and-rings, up to 42 cm ($16\frac{1}{2}$ in) diameter, having up to 5 rings, some incomplete or gapped, others complete, some with,

some without, a radial groove from the cup, also 16 cups. Greatest carving depth 1 cm ($\frac{1}{2}$ in).

Coles had been informed of these carvings by a man who had seen them 50 years earlier. But neither Coles nor this man seem to have been able to locate them again, stating they were 'near North Balfern gate'. The sketch produced by Coles (reproduced here) was said to be 'only a very rough one' and may have been based on a memory of 50 years earlier. As it is so different and includes a rare 2-ended spiral, the author has searched diligently for another set of carvings here, but without success, and they possibly are all the same.

NORTH BALFERN — looking W.

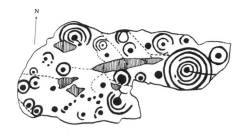

NORTH BALFERN   Scale 3:100.

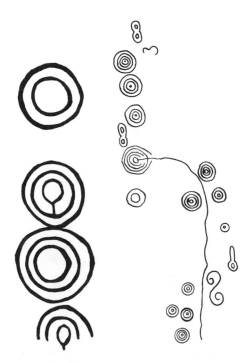

NORTH BALFERN — the "rough diagram, made from memory" produced to F. R. Coles in 1901. The carvings are so different, yet no other site has been found in recent times, near the house's gate.

Stevenson 1947, p. 129–130
Stevenson 1948, p. 208
Cannon 1948, p. 244
Simpson & Thawley 1972, pp. 91 & 101

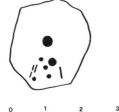

Cist-cover found 350 m SE of the farm, 4 km W of Wigtown, 4½ km inland, in pasture. First reported by R. B. K. Stevenson (1947).

NX 392 557 OS: old 80 and Wigtown 21 SW; new 83 and NX 35 NE. 20 m (70 ft).

125 m (135 yds) SSW of road B733 was a stone cist. Its roughly hexagonal greywacke cover-slab, ¾ m by ¾ m by 10 cm (2½ ft × 2¼ ft × 4 in) was carved on both sides –

(a) Facing outwards – 6 'cups' and perhaps 3 incised grooves.

(b) Facing inwards – 5 'cups', about 16 incised grooves and scratches, and a very faintly scratched pattern of 3 diamonds.

There is also a hole completely through the centre of the stone, narrowing on both sides as it goes in. Many of these markings probably were made in industrial use. But some on the inner face (e.g. the 'diamonds') probably were not.

Left: REDBRAE — the 2 sides of this cist-cover. The central "cup" goes right through the stone.

REDBRAE — the cist-cover's outer face. The spectacles at the bottom left give scale.

ST. NINIAN'S CAVE

Small slabs found near the cave, 5 km SSW of Whithorn, at sea edge, on fossilised upper beach. First reported by the Royal Commission on Ancient Monuments of Scotland (1914).

K. Inventory 1914, no. 3

NX 422 359 OS: old 80 and Wigtown 35 SE; new 83 and NX 43 NW. 12 m (40 ft).

From the existence of the cup-and-ring symbol in a crannog (**AYR 7 – Lochlee**), and in souterrains in Angus, all of which uses date from a date AD, it might be argued that the slabs mentioned below are examples of the old symbol being 'grafted' on to the new faith's symbol to reinforce it, as has been done in other faiths. But Mr. R. B. K. Stevenson, until recently keeper of the National Museum of Antiquities of Scotland, who is probably the leading authority on Scottish Early Christian carvings, writes –

Letter to the author, 8th February 1977

'I feel quite sure the resemblance is quite accidental. The intention was to copy a Cross marked out by compasses or dividers, one diameter for the outer ends and four smaller circles for the arms (he was discussing the first example mentioned below). When properly done there should be gaps, but often the small circles are completed. Dot-and-circle decoration was very common at the same and many other periods, when compasses were in frequent use.... In the angles of the Cross you often get bosses in relief, some with a depression in the centre. The stone from the cave is a simple version.'

Mr. Stevenson has also stated that, while the Cross itself in early Christian days represented the *physical* crucifixion, the symbols at the four points of the Cross and at its centre, with perhaps no actual Cross outlined, represented the *spiritual* side of the resurrection.

Dalrymple Lectures, Glasgow, 1977

The stones are shown here, however, as this question of the dual symbolism may well be raised again, when Mr. Stevenson's opinion on the matter may be useful. 2 slabs from near the cave, both now in the Priory Museum, Whithorn, merit examination –

(a) About ½ m by ½ m (1½ ft × 1½ ft), no 7. On it are 4 complete cups-and-one-ring arranged as the 4 points of a Cross, all inside a large ring 26 cm (10 in) diameter, with a small cup-mark in its centre.

(b) About 35 cm by 15 cm (14 in × 6 in), no 16. On it is a Cross having in its centre a very well-preserved cup-and-one-complete-ring 5 cm (2 in) diameter.
See also **GAL 43**.

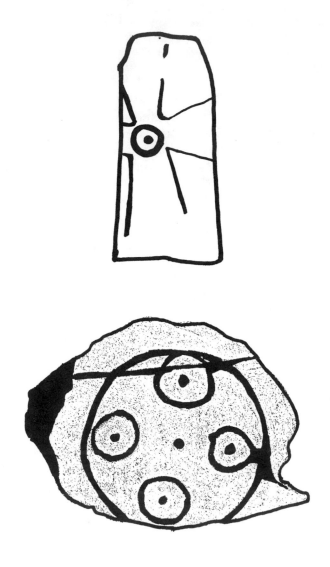

ST. NINIAN's CAVE — 2 of the Early Christian Crosses, now in the Priory Museum, Whithorn. Was the cup-and-ring symbol here "grafted on" to the Cross to reinforce the new Faith. Or was its use purely accidental and ornamental? Mr. R. B. K. Stevenson, the leading authority on Early Scottish Crosses, thinks the latter was undoubtedly the case.

SENWICK 1

GAL 100

Outcrop 140 m E of Senwick House, 2½ km SE of Borgue, 1 km inland, sea views, in pasture. First reported by F. R. Coles (1894).

Coles 1894, p. 72
K. Inventory 1914, no. 248
Morris & Bailey 1964, p. 167
Morris 1966, p. 114

NX 6472 4668 OS: old 80 and Kirkcudbright 54 SE; new 83 and NX 64 NW. 48 m (160 ft).

270 m (300 yds) NNE of the wall at the road junction, 110 m (120 yds) ESE of the nearest road wall, just SE of 2 prominent boulders, is a greywacke outcrop area about 13 m by 2 m, up to 1¼ m high on its N (42 ft × 6 ft × 4 ft), turfed in parts. On it are 2 groups 2 m (6 ft) apart, on horizontal surfaces, all much weathered –

(a) On the NE area – 3 cups-and-two-rings, 1 cup-and-one-ring, and at least 6 cups. Some rings are gapped, some complete, and one has a radial groove from its cup.

(b) On the SW area – 2 cups-and-one-complete-ring and 3 cups.

The greatest ring diameter is 20 cm (8 in) and carving depths up to 3 cm (1¼ in).

Coles' diagram of 1894 differs from the above description.

SENWICK 1 — looking E.

SENWICK 1 — some of the carvings, looking S.E.

SENWICK 1 — N.E. part. Scale 3:100.   SENWICK 1 — S.W. part. Scale 3:100.

SENWICK 2

GAL 101

Outcrop 450 m S of Senwick House, 2½ km SE of Borgue, 1 km inland, sea views, in pasture. First reported by F. R. Coles (1894).

Coles 1894, p. 88
K. Inventory 1914, no. 67
Morris & Bailey 1964, p. 164
Morris 1966, p. 114

NX 6446 4620 OS: old 80 and Kirkcudbright 54SE, new 83 and NX 64 NW 30 m (100 ft).

In the next field S of the Brighouse road, 23 m (25 yds) SE of the road wall, 113 m (125 yds) S of a gate opposite the keeper's house, was an outcrop ½ m by ½ m at ground level (1½ ft × 1½ ft), sloping 5° N. On it the Royal Commission on Ancient Monuments of Scotland and the Ordnance Survey noted –

A much-weathered cup-and-one-ring 18 cm (7 in) diameter, probably complete, ¼ cm (⅛ in) deep. Coles noted a cup-and-four-rings in 1894 on what was probably the same site. The author has been unable to trace this site.

SENWICK 3

GAL 102

Rock (outcrop?) about 700 m S of Senwick House, 2½ km SE of Borgue 1 km inland, sea views, in pasture. First reported by F. R. Coles (1894) at present un-traceable.

Coles 1894, p. 88
K. Inventory 1914, no. 67
Morris & Bailey 1964, p. 164
Morris 1966, p 114

NX 644 459 OS: old 80 and Kirkcudbright 54 SE; new 83 and NX 64 NW 45 m (150 ft).

'About 300 yds (270 m) further South and 50 ft (15 m) higher up, only a few feet from a dyke (wall) running ENE' (possibly the Windryridge road wall) Coles noted –

2 cups-and-one-complete-ring and 10 cups (no measurements are given).

This has not been seen since at least 1911, and may well be under turf.

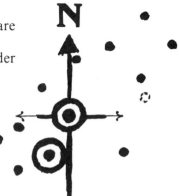

SENWICK 3 — F. R. Coles' diagram of this set of carvings, now missing. Scale unknown.

GAL 103

TONGUE CROFT

*Morris & Bailey 1964,
p. 164 & plate XXII
Morris 1966, p. 114*

Outcrop 600 m W of Ingliston farm, 3 km W of Borgue, $\frac{1}{2}$ km inland, sea views, in pasture. First reported by the author (1964).

NX 6033 4833 OS: old 80 and Kirkcudbright 54 SW; new 83 and NX 64 NW. 15 m (50 ft).

11 m (12 yds) S of the road's wall, $4\frac{1}{2}$ m (5 yds) NW of a small stream, 1 m (yd) S of a telegraph pole, are 3 adjoining greywacke outcrops, in all $7\frac{1}{2}$ m by $4\frac{1}{2}$ m, up to $\frac{3}{4}$ m high on their S (25 ft × 15 ft × $2\frac{1}{2}$ ft). On the eastmost 2 parts are –

(a) On the centre part, sloping 15°E, a cup-and-six-complete-rings with 2 radial grooves from its cup, a natural triangle surrounded by 2 rings and a very faint cup-and-one-ring.

(b) On the E (lower) part, sloping 5°E, is a cup-and-three-complete-rings.

Greatest ring diameter – 35 cm (14 in) and carving depths up to 1 cm ($\frac{1}{2}$ in).

TONGUE CROFT — looking S.W.

TORRS 1   GAL 104

Outcrop 15 m N of farm, 6 km S of Kirkcudbright, 1 km inland, sea views, in rubbish dump (former pasture). First reported by F. R. Coles (1894).

NX 6802 4586 OS: old 80 and Kirkcudbright 55 SW; new 83 and NX 64 NE. 45 m (150 ft).

Coles 1894, p. 88
K. Inventory 1914, no. 67
Morris & Bailey 1964, p. 164
Morris 1966, p. 114

15 m (17 yds) N of the byre's gable, in a rubbish dump among much old timber, is a smoothish greywacke area, cleared by the author for ¾ m by ½ m (2½ ft × 1¾ ft) about 5 cm (2 in) below ground level, sloping 5°NNW. On it are –

10 cups enclosed by, or among, grooves, including 2 irregular 'dented ovals' up to 53 cm (21 in) diameters – carvings up to 2 cm (1 in) deep.

70 cm (2¼ ft) E of this, Coles found 2 cup-marks; but the author was unsuccessful in finding these under the rubbish.

1 m (3 ft) S of it in 1911 was noted a 'vague nearly complete ring with a cup in its centre'. The author was also unsuccessful in uncovering this, on 3 visits.

Right: TORRS 1 — looking towards the farm's byre.

TORRS 1 — the unusual carvings on this rock, looking S.

Outcrops around 14 m N of the farm, 6 km S of Kirkcudbright, 1 km inland, sea views, in rough grass. First reported by F. R. Coles (1894).

Coles 1894, p. 72–73
K. Inventory 1914, no. 148
Morris & Bailey 1964, p. 167
Morris 1966, p. 114

NX 6805 4586 OS: same sheets and altitude as GAL 104.

On a low knoll, 26 m (29 yds) E of **GAL 104**, a greywacke area 14 m by 9 m (45 ft × 30 ft) has at its summit, about 7 cm ($\frac{1}{4}$ ft) above the rest of its rough surface, a smooth area. On this, sloping 10° E are –

3 cups-and-four-mostly-complete-rings, up to 23 cm (9 in) diameters, with grooves from each outer ring connecting them like a 'Prince-of-Wales' feathers', except that the centre groove begins at the cup and stops just short of the others in a cup-mark – all a most striking design. Greatest carrving depth – 1 cm ($\frac{1}{2}$ in).

4 m (13 ft) SW of this, on the same knoll, is a cup-and-two-complete-rings 15 cm (6 in) diameter, of negligible depth, first noted by the author, in 1973.

6 m (20 ft) W of the 'Feathers', there was noted 'on the same rock', 2 small cups, N and S of each other, surrounded by small dots as if an attempt to put a groove round them had been abandoned. This group could not be traced in 1964–78.

'$2\frac{1}{2}$ m ($8\frac{1}{2}$ ft) ESE' of this last group, were noted in 1894 a completely un-weathered cup-and-two-rings 21 cm ($8\frac{1}{2}$ in) diameter, and a cup – both in a squarish rock hollow, no doubt now turf-covered. It has not been seen since before 1911.

TORRS 2 — the main site, looking S.W. towards the farm.

TORRS 2 — the interesting "Prince of Wales' Feathers" pattern formed by the carvings. One of the very few attempts at design among these early Scottish carvings.

TORRS 2 — the carvings chalked in, except that a very faint fourth ring, later noted on the right, is not shown.

TORRS 2 — the newly-discovered very much weathered cup-and-ring chalked in.

GAL 106

TORRS 3

Outcrop 600 m SSW of the farm, $3\frac{1}{2}$ km S of Kirkcudbright, $\frac{1}{2}$ km inland, sea views from near, in pasture. First reported by F. R. Coles (1894).

Coles 1894, p. 71
K. Inventory 1914, no. 248
Morris & Bailey 1964, p. 167
Morris 1966, p. 114

NX 6792 4522 OS: same sheets as GAL 104. 40 m (140 ft).

(a) In 1894 Coles noted somewhere on the Well Hill, 'near the Ewe Buchts' (the sheepfold which now contains an Army hutment) –

Many shallow cups 2 cm (1 in) wide 'scattered about; a groove follows the edge of the rock and connects 2 cups, one of which is surrounded by a ring'.

It is thought this could not be traced by the Royal Commission on Ancient Monuments of Scotland in 1911, and no trace could be found on several visits in 1964–1975. But in searching, the late D. C. Bailey, in 1964, first noted –

(b) 55 m (60 yds) WSW of the W corner of the sheepfold, a grey-wacke outcrope and turf ridge, here outcropping for $4\frac{3}{4}$ m by $\frac{3}{4}$ m and up to $\frac{1}{4}$ m high (15 ft $\times$ $2\frac{1}{2}$ ft $\times$ $\frac{3}{4}$ ft). On its fairly smooth surface, where sloping 10°N are –

Morris & Bailey 1964,
p. 167
Morris 1966, p. 114

A well-preserved cup-and-one-complete-ring with 3 radial grooves from the ring, one a long one leading downhill, also a cup-mark. Ring diameter – 12 cm (5 in) and greatest carving depth – 3 cm (1 in).

See also under **GAL 77** – Knockshinnie – which hill is part of Torrs farm.

TORRS 3 — the carvings, looking S.W.

TORRS 3 — a recently-discovered site, looking N.N.E., towards the farm.

Outcrop 950 m NNW of the farm, 4½ km SSE of Kirkcudbright, 2 km inland; sea views, in pasture. First noted by the author (1973).

NX 6932 4718 OS: old 80 and Kirkcudbright 55 SW; new 83 and NX 64 NE. 115 m (380 ft).

55 m (60 yds) E of the gate into the third field along the track, 80 m (90 yds) N of the now felled Townhead wood, is a mostly horizontal greywacke outcrop 10 m by 4½ m up to 15 cm high (33 ft × 15 ft × ½ ft) divided by turf. On it are –

At least 13 cups-and-rings, some of irregular shapes, some gapped, un-gapped, and incomplete, some in associated groups, and in one case a ring surrounding 2 cups. There are from 1 to 5 concentric rings, up to 45 cm (17 in) diameters and also at least 10 cups. Greatest carving depth 3 cm (1 in). Further excavation may reveal more carvings.

This is one of the most varied and interesting outcrop sites in Galloway. It merits careful preservation.

TOWNHEAD 1 — the W. half, looking S.E.

TOWNHEAD 1 — the E half, looking S.E.

TOWNHEAD 1 — looking W, towards the field's entrance gate.

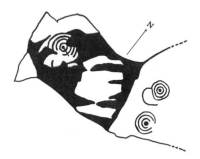

TOWNHEAD 1 — the W half. Scale 3:100.   TOWNHEAD 1 — the E half. Scale 3:100.

TOWNHEAD 2   GAL 108

Outcrops 850 m NNW of the farm, in similar situation as last above. First reported by the author (1973).

NX 6947 4712 OS: old 80 and Kirkcudbright 55 SE; new 83 and NX 64 NE. 110 m (360 ft).

In the same original field, now divided by a temporary fence, is a knoll and quarry, 58 m (63 yds) NNW of a gate. 8 m (9 yds) S of its sloping face are some greywacke stones or outcrops –

(a) A barrel-shaped stone $1\frac{1}{4}$ m by $\frac{3}{4}$ m, $\frac{3}{4}$ m high on its SE, but at ground level on its W (4 ft × $2\frac{1}{2}$ ft × $2\frac{1}{2}$ ft). On a horizontal part of it is –

A cup-and-four-complete-rings 24 cm (9 in) diameter, and a small cup, both of negligible depth.

(b) 1 m (yd) SE of it is a cup-marked stone sloping 10°S with a few irregular grooves on it, 1 m by $\frac{3}{4}$ m by $\frac{1}{4}$ m (3$\frac{1}{2}$ ft × 2$\frac{1}{2}$ ft × 1 ft).

(c) 5$\frac{1}{2}$ m (6 yds) NW of (a) is a domed stone, $\frac{3}{4}$ m by $\frac{1}{2}$ m, $\frac{1}{8}$ m high (2$\frac{3}{4}$ ft × 2 ft × $\frac{1}{2}$ ft). On it, where the slope is about 10°SSW is –

A cup-and-seven-rings 38 cm (15 in) diameter. Some rings are complete, others gapped, or incomplete where they meet the stone's edge. 2 of the rings end in a cup at each side. Greatest carving depth – $\frac{1}{2}$ cm ($\frac{1}{8}$ in).

All the carvings on this site are very much weathered and only visible in low sun or when wet.

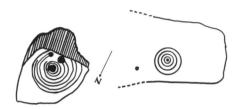

TOWNHEAD 2 — the W stone. The E. Stone. Scale 3:100.

TOWNHEAD 2 — One of the stones chalked in, (the chalked-in lines on R. of the stone do not represent carving, only a steep gradient and rough surface).

TOWNHEAD 2 — the E, barrel-shaped, stone. More cup-marks may be discovered here when seen in different light conditions.

TOWNHEAD 2 — the W. stone, looking S.S.E. The 7 much-weathered rings can just be seen.

Outcrops 900 m NNW of the farm, $4\frac{1}{2}$ km SSE of Kirkcudbright, 2 km inland, sea views, in pasture. First reported by the author (1973).

NX 6941 4713 OS: old 80 and Kirkcudbright 55 SW; new 83 and NX 64 NE. 112 m (370 ft).

In the same field, 45 m (50 yds) E of the gate in the temporary fence dividing it in two in 1973; 180 m (200 yds) E of **GAL 107**, 135 m (150 yds) WNW of **GAL 108**, are 2 greywacke outcrops at ground level, hard to find, 3 m (yds) apart.

(a) On the NW slab, $1\frac{1}{2}$ m by $\frac{3}{4}$ m (5 ft × $2\frac{1}{4}$ ft) sloping 5°S, are –

A cup-and-two-complete-rings 15 cm (6 in) diameter and 14 cups, some connected by grooves, all of negligible depth.

(b) 3 m ($3\frac{1}{3}$ yds) SE, on a surface $1\frac{1}{4}$ m by 1 m (4 ft × 3 ft) sloping 5°E, are –

12 cups (2 with 'tails') and 3 grooves which seem like the beginnings of an attempted flattened cup-and-two-rings. There is also a natural 'hole'.

Further excavation in this field may reveal other sites. In 1964 the late D. C. Bailey reported 4 sites here, and although his description of each is very different from those given above, and he was unable to re-locate them on two later visits with the author, at least one of them may be the same as one of the above.

TOWNHEAD 3 — the N.W. stone, looking S.S.E.

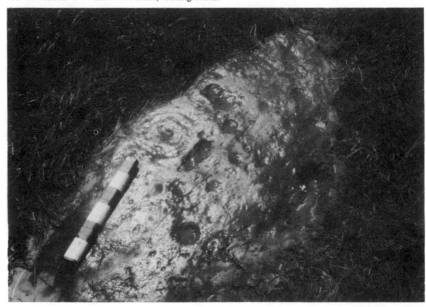

TOWNHEAD 3 — the S.E. stone, looking S.S.E.

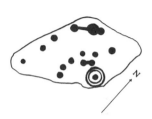 

TOWNHEAD 3 — Scale 3:100.

GAL 110   UPPER NEWTON

Small slab found on the farm, about 3 km SW of Anwoth, ½ km inland. First reported by the Royal Commission on Ancient Monuments of Scotland (1914).

NX 55 55 OS: old 80; new 83 and NX 55 NE.

K. Inventory 1914, no. 20
Morris & Bailey 1964, p. 164 & plate XXII
Morris 1966, p. 114

Flat greywacke slab ½ m by ¼ m by 8 cm (2 ft × ¾ ft × ¼ ft) now cemented into the garden shed behind Kirkdale House (NX 515 533). On it are –

11 cups-and-one-complete-ring, some broken off at the stone's edges, up to 9 cm (3½ in) diameters, and at least 3 cups. The cups are unusually large for so small rings. Greatest carving depth – 1 cm (½ in).

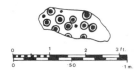

UPPER NEWTON — the slab from this farm, now in the garden at Kirkdale House.

WHITHORN GOLF COURSE GAL 111

Outcrop chip found on the golf course 2½ km inland, on former moor – sea views – now missing. Reported by the Rev. R. S. G. Anderson (1926).

NX 452 401 OS: old 80 and Wigtown 31SE and 35NE; new 83 and NX 44 SW. About 60 m (200 ft).

Anderson 1926, p. 121

The Rev. R. S. G. Anderson reported being shown 'a small fragment of stone..., picked up on the "Duck's Back" green.... Possibly the horse-mower had chipped it off an outcrop and deposited it (on the green)' some distance away. This green was about 440 m (480 yds) NNE of High Skeog road and 10 m (11 yds) W of a wall. The chip was 4 cm by 3½ cm by 1 cm (1½ in × 1⅜ in × ½ in). On it were –

'2 rings and possibly a third'. No mention is made of a cup, on this small fragment.

WHITHORN PRIORY MUSEUM GAL 112

Small slab, of unknown provenance, held in the Museum.

NX 444 403 OS: old 80; new 83.

There is a slab in the Museum, believed to have been found on the former Whithorn golf course. It measures ½ m by ⅓ m by 10 cm (1½ ft × 1 ft × 4 in). On its flat surface are –

Morris & Bailey 1964, p. 172 & plate XXI Morris 1966, p. 116

4 concentric rings, 25 cm (10 in) diameter, up to 1 cm (½ in) deep. There is no cup-mark.

Another stone, formerly in the Museum, is now in the Kirkcudbright Museum – **GAL 14**.

MAN ~ The Isle of Man

In the Isle of Man there are many examples of the same site being used again and again for different cultures. As will be seen below, this re-use seems to have occurred in several of the sites listed.

BALLAGAWNE KEILL   MAN 1

Slab found in the keeill or chapel, 5 km NW of Castletown, 3 km inland; now in the Manx Museum, Douglas. First reported by Canon Savage (about 1880).

SC 2395 7187 OS: old 87 and 16; new 95 and SC 27 SW. 110 m (260 ft).

Kermode 1925, p. 128
Bruce 1968, p. 36 and plate XVII

Gritstone slab, 1 m by $\frac{1}{2}$ m by $\frac{1}{4}$ m (3 ft × 1$\frac{1}{2}$ ft × $\frac{3}{4}$ ft) found at the chapel. On its flat surface are –

A shallow basin 25 cm diameter, 5 cm deep (9 in × 2 in) and at least 14 cups. 10 of these are arranged in 3 rows below the basin. The other 3 are just above it.

It has been suggested that this may be a gaming stone of later date. But a similar arrangement of cups is also found in various sites in Britain associated with cups-and-rings – for example at Gourock in W. Scotland.

Morris 1967, p. 78

BALLAGAWNE KEEILL — a copy of J. R. Bruce's photograph in the Manx Archaeological Survey, by his and their kind permission. This stone is now stored in the Manx Museum.

BALLARAGH

Slab in road wall, 50 m W of the farm, 1¾ km NE of Laxey, ½ km inland, in pasture, sea views. First reported by P. M. C. Kermode (1930). (1930).

SC 452 855 OS: old 87 and 8; new 95 and SC 48 NE. 200 m (650 ft).

Kermode 1930, p. 52
Daniel 1950, p. 60 & 117
Megaw 1945, p. 225
Walker 1970, p. 57
Manx Museum 1973, p. 33

Granite slab, now built into the roadway B11's WNW wall, said to have been one of a group of stones which had to be moved in road construction – 1¼ m by 1 m (4 ft × 3 ft). On its nearly vertical, fairly smooth, surface, about 10 cm (6 in) from the bottom as now uncovered, are –

The much-weathered remains of at least 3 spirals in line, with carved lines above and below which suggest that other 2 spirals may have existed there. Each probably had 2 to 3 convolutions, diameters only about 5 cm (2 in). Greatest carving depth ⅛ cm (1/16 in). Total carved area only about 25 cm by 20 cm (10 in × 8 in).

Some have suggested this may be part of a megalithic structure or stone coffin (cist). A few doubt its antiquity. No spirals of so small a diameter have been found, to the author's knowledge, in Scotland. The carvings have been incised, not, as is more usual, pecked.

BALLARAGH — the "spiral stone". The 3 spirals which are in line are chalked in at the bottom of the stone.

BALLARAGH — scale 1:10 (in view of the very small size of this carving.) The dotted lines do not exist, but they show how the figure **may** once have been completed.

BALLARAGH — the spirals.

Slab found at the chapel, 1 km NE of Crosby, 6½ km inland, in pasture. First reported by Mr. Shaw (1877).

SC 332 802 OS: old 87 and 10 ; new 95 and SC 38 SW. 115 m (380 ft).

Shaw 1877, p. 53

Standing stone, found in the surrounding wall of the chapel. On its flat surface Shaw's guidebook says there were –

A cup-and-two-rings, and below it three concentric rings. All rings were complete.

Shaw's Guidebook says this was 'one of several stones inscribed with various designs and inscriptions' in the wall. It and the others are now missing. But possibly, if the Guidebook's picture is inaccurate, this may be the same stone as **MAN 4**.

KEEILL VREESHEY (HOLY BRIDGET CHAPEL) — from Shaw's sketch.

In addition to MAN 1, and 5, the Museum houses 2 stones of unknown provenance gifted to it, now in its store –

MAN 4 – Gritstone slab, said to have been found in the Glen Vine area (i.e. quite near where **MAN 3** was), gifted to the Museum, measuring $\frac{3}{4}$ m by $\frac{1}{3}$ m by $\frac{1}{4}$ m ($2\frac{1}{2}$ ft × 1 ft × $\frac{3}{4}$ ft). On its smooth flat surface, rather near one end, are –

A cup-and-two-complete-rings 20 cm diameter and up to 1 cm deep (8 in × $\frac{1}{2}$ in), a much-weathered cup-and-one-complete-ring with a long radial groove from the ring to the end of the stone, and a broken-off half-circle.

From the carvings' positions, this might well have been a standing stone, and possibly the same as the now missing **MAN 3**.

MANX MUSEUM — stone, possibly from KEEILL VREESHEY
(Holy Bridget Chapel) now stored in the Museum.

MANX MUSEUM — stone, probably from Ballaglonny, now stored in the Museum.

MAN 5 – Gritstone slab 1½ m by 1 m by ½ m (5 ft × 3 ft × 1½ ft). On its smooth flat surface are –

A ring 23 cm (9 in) diameter, inside which are a rosette of 8 cups and a central cup, all much weathered. This is a design also found in other parts of the British Isles, for example at **ARG 71**, Ormaig, in Argyll. There are also at least 11 cups; and at least 3 of these have traces of being surrounded by one complete ring, with, in one case, traces of a second, much bigger, ring tangental to the 23 cm ring. Another has a radial groove from ring to stone's edge.

It has been suggested at the Museum that this may be the stone found by Sir James Simpson or his daughter Mrs. Blyth about 1867 on Ballaglonny farm (*SC 30 72*), but this is uncertain.

Un-reported

Morris 1977

SULBRICK

Slab in the keeill (chapel), 7½ km W of Douglas, 4½ km inland. First reported by P. M. C. Kermode (1918).

SC 309 746 OS: old 87 and 13; new 95 and SC 37 SW. 90 m (300 ft).

Granite slab, 1 m by ½ m by 10 cm (3 ft × 1½ ft × 4 in) found placed against the altar's front, carved side towards the altar. On its flat side are –

A roughly hexagonal 'ring'. Inside this are a number of straight and curved grooves, whose pattern is not discernable, and which are unlike any Scottish prehistoric carving known to the author.

The stone has been replaced in position and re-covered. Those who have seen it suggest it may be pre-Christian – a prehistoric revered carving placed in this Early Christian site. But it may well be of a different age or series from the other carvings listed here.

Megaw 1932, p. 22 & plate 173(7)

Kermode 1918, p. 22 & plate XXIII

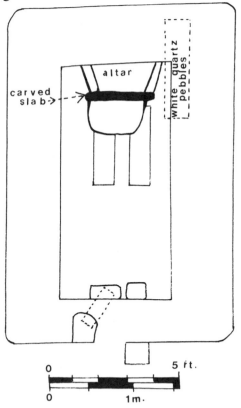

Left: SUBRICK KEEILL — the slab, placed against the altar in the Keeill, now re-covered there. From P. M. C. Kermode's photograph in the Manx Archaeological Survey, by their kind permission.

Right: SULBRICK KEEILL (chapel) — sketch plan, showing where the carved slab was found (and replaced) — face inwards, against the altar. (after P. M. C. Kermode.)

GALLOWAY

Accessible sites you may care to visit:
If you are in the *West of Galloway* – in Wigtown district – with only a short time to spare, and do not want to walk far, you might visit any or all of GAL 51, 2, **47–49**, 75, **112**, 52, 24 and 97, in that order from West to East – House of Elrig, Balcraig 2, **Drumtroddan**, Knock 1, **Whithorn Priory Museum** (which shows, besides a slab of unknown provenance, 2 cross-slabs GAL 99 from St. Ninian's Cave), Gallows Outon, Broughton Mains 2, and North Balfern.

Further East, between Newton Stewart and Gatehouse of Fleet, again travelling East, you may care to visit all or any of GAL 72, **71**, 12 and 26 – Kirkmabreck, **Kirkdale House** (housing 6 stones) Barholm 2, and Cairnholy 2 (spectacular chamber tomb, but very worn carving, visible only around noon). With half a day to spare, a walk over the lovely moors behind Creetown will bring you to the big spiral at GAL 32 and also to GAL 25 – Cambret Moor and Cairnharrow.

There are 2 stones in **Kirkcudbright's Museum** – GAL 14 and 78. The area just South and East of Kirkcudbright is probably the best area for finding these cup-and-ring carvings –

Going South in Galloway, you'll find GAL 60 and 104 and 105 Grange and Torrs 1 and 2. A little further on, taking the car as far as you can up the farm road, a fairly short walk will bring you to GAL 13 and **107**, both well worth a visit – Blackhill and **Townhead 1**. Unless you have Army permission, do not try to visit the sites here which I have stated are in the Heavy Weapons Practice Range or you may find yourself, as I did once, being shelled by artillery.

East of Kirkcudbright, you must look at GAL **63**, 21 and **94**. The last of these entails a walk uphill, but, although it is a little hard to find, it is one of the most deeply carved stones and well worth the effort to find it – **High Banks**, Bombie and **Newlaw Hill 1**. GAL 89 – Milton 3 – is also easily got at, but is a small carving.

THE ISLE OF MAN

In the **Isle of Man**, you can without difficulty see MAN 1 – Ballargh – on the roadside, and MAN 3, 4 and 5 in the store in the Manx Museum in Douglas.

BIBLIOGRAPHY

GALLOWAY

Anderson 1921	Rev. R. S. G. Anderson's 'Rock Sculpture at Gallows Outon' in *PSAS* LIV (1921–1922).
Anderson 1926	Rev. R. S. G. Anderson's 'Crosses and Rock Sculptures in Wigtownshire' in *PSAS* LXI (1926–1927).
Anderson 1930(1)	Rev. R. S. G. Anderson's photographs now in the Stranraer Museum, gifted in 1930.
Anderson 1930(2)	Rev. R. S. G. Anderson's 'Two cups-and-rings in the Stewartry' in *TG & DNHS* XIV (1926–1930).
Breuil 1934	H. Breuil's Presidential Address in *PPS* 1934.
Cannon 1948	J. Cannon's presentation mentioned in *PSAS* LXXXIII (1948–1949).
Coles 1894	F. R. Coles 'Cup-and-ring markings in Kirkcudbright' in *PSAS* XXIX (1894–1895).
Coles 1898	F. R. Coles' 'Cup-and-ring-marked stones' in *PSAS* XXXII (1898–1899).
Coles 1902	F. R. Coles' 'Cup-and-ring marked stones' in *PSAS* XXXVII (1902–1903).
Coles 1905	F. R. Coles' 'Cup-and-ring markings' in *PSAS* XL 1905–1906).
Coles' sketches	F. R. Coles' plans of carvings deposited with the Stewartry Museum, Kirkcudbright.
Crawford 1957	O. G. S. Crawford's *The Eye Goddess* (1957).
D & E	*Discovery and Excavation, Scotland.*
Feachem 1963	R. W. Feachem's *Guide to Prehistoric Scotland* 1963.
Ferguson 1961	A. Ferguson in *D. & E.* (1961).
Flett 1926	D. Flett's '2 cup-&-ring stones in the Stewartry' in *TG & DNHS* (1926–1928).
HBNC	'History of the Berwickshire Naturalists' Club'.
Hadingham 1974	E. Hadingham's *Ancient Carvings in Britain* (1974).
Hadingham 1975	E. Hadingham's *Circles and Standing Stones* (1975)
Hamilton 1886	G. Hamilton's 'Ancient Sculpturings in Kirkcudbrightshire' in *PSAS* XXI (1886–1887).
Hamilton 1888	G. Hamilton's 'Additional . . . Carvings at High Banks' in *PSAS* XXIII (1888–1889).
K. Inventory 1914	Royal Commission on Ancient and Historical Monuments of Scotland's Inventory of Kirkcudbrightshire (1914).
W. Inventory 1912	Royal Commission on Ancient and Historical Monuments of Scotland's Inventory of Wigtownshire (1912).
JRSAI	*Journal of the Royal Society of Antiquaries of Ireland.*
Mackenzie 1841	W. Mackenzie's *History of Galloway* vol. 2 (1841, J. Nicholson).
Maclagan 1933	D. P. Maclagan's presentation, mentioned in *PSAS* LXVIII (1933–1934).

Maclagan 1937	D. P. Maclagan's presentation, mentioned in *PSAS* LXXII (1937–1938).
Macleod 1969	I. F. Macleod in D & E 1969.
McWhite 1946	E. McWhite in *JRSAI* LXXVI (1946).
Mann 1938	L. M. Mann's *Earliest Glasgow* (1938).
Mann 1915	L. M. Mann's *Archaic Sculptures* (1915).
Maxwell 1900	Sir Herbert Maxwell's presentation, in *PSAS* XXXV (1900–1901).
Morris 1964	R. B. M. Morris in *TAMS* 12 (1964).
Morris & Bailey 1964	R. W. B. Morris & D. C. Bailey's 'Cup-and-ring marks of S.W. Scotland' in *PSAS* XCVIII (1964–1966).
Morris 1966	R. W. B. Morris 'Cup-and-ring marks of S. W. Scotland' in *TAMS* 14 (1966–1967).
Morris 1967	R. W. B. Morris' 'Cup-and-ring marks' in *PSAS* 100 (1967–1968).
Morris 1969	R. W. B. Morris' 'Cup-and-ring marks' in *TAMS* 16 (1968–1969).
Morris 1973	R. W. B. Morris' 'Prehistoric Petroglyphs of Southern Scotland' in *Bollettino di Studi Prehistorici*, 10 (1973).
Morris 1977	R. W. B. Morris' *The Prehistoric Rock Art of Argyll* (1977).
Paturi 1976	F. R. Paturi's *Zeugender der Vorzeit* (Vienna 1976 – in German).
Piggott & Powell 1948	S. Piggott and T. G. E. Powell's 'Excavation of three megalithic chambered tombs' in *PSAS* LXXXIII 1948–1949).
PSAS	*The Proceedings of the Society of Antiquaries of Scotland.*
PPS	*The Proceedings of the Prehistoric Society of East Anglia (now the Prehistoric Society).*
Statistical Account 1965	*Third Statistical Account of Scotland* vol. on 'Kirkcudbright & Wigtown' (1965).
Simpson 1864	Sir James Simpson in *PSAS* VI (1864–1865) Appendix.
Simpson 1867	Sir James Simpson's *Archaic Sculptures* (1867).
Simpson & Thawley 1972	D. D. A. Simpson & J. A. Thawley's 'Single Grave Art in Britain' in *Scottish Archaeological Forum* (1972).
Stevenson 1926	R. B. K. Stevenson in *TG & DNHS* XIV (1926–1928).
Stevenson 1947	R. B. K. Stevenson in *TG & DNHS* XXVI (1947–1948).
Stevenson 1948	R. B. K. Stevenson in *TG & DNHS* XXVII (1948–1949).
Stuart 1856	J. Stuart's *Sculptured Stones of Scotland* (1856).
Scott 1951	Sir Lindsay Scott's 'The Colonisation of Scotland in the Second Millennium BC' in *PPS* XVII (1951).
SR	Special Reports on the Mineral Resources of Scotland.
TAMS	*Transactions of the Ancient Monuments Society.*
TBNC	*Transactions of the Berwickshire Naturalists' Club.*
TG & DNHS	*Transactions of the Galloway and Dumfriesshire Natural History and Antiquarian Society.*
Thom 1967	A. Thom's *Megalithic Sites in Britain* (1967).
Thom 1968	A. Thom in *TAMS* – 'The Geometry of Cup-and-Ring Marks'